17.45

WordPerfect

for beginners

Louise Benzer

First Printing, 1991
Printed in U.S.A.

Copyright © 1991 Abacus
          5370 52nd Street, SE
          Grand Rapids, MI 49512

```
Library of Congress Cataloging-in-Publication Data
Benzer, Louise, 1966-
WordPerfect for beginners / Louise Benzer.
      p.   cm.
Includes index.
ISBN 1-55755-117-0
      1. WordPerfect (Computer program)
      2. Word processing - Computer
         programs. I. Title.
Z52.5.W65B48   1991
652.5'536- -dc20                        91-20153
                                            CIP
```

Introduction

As you probably already know, WordPerfect, from the WordPerfect Corporation, is one of the most flexible and powerful word processing programs available. Besides enabling you to create and edit text on a computer, WordPerfect also includes math, graphics and mail merge capabilities. However, in order to use WordPerfect effectively, you must know how to use its many features.

Although this may seem overwhelming at first, with *WordPerfect for Beginners* you'll master the basics of the WordPerfect program quickly, so you can create a variety of documents immediately.

This book is designed for people who have little or no experience using WordPerfect. Starting from the most basic actions, we gradually move on to more advanced procedures, building on what you've learned. We also include examples that correspond to the explanations. So, as you move through the book you can actually practice using what you've learned.

Also, since this book is designed for beginners, we've tried to keep technical terms and confusing computerese to a minimum. Because of this, we encourage you to refer to your WordPerfect manual if you ever need more information on a topic.

Using this book
The procedures described in this book were performed using Version 5.1 of WordPerfect, which was installed on the hard drive of a computer and WordPerfect was located in the C:\WP51 subdirectory. If you haven't installed WordPerfect on your hard drive yet or don't have a hard drive, refer to your WordPerfect manual for instructions.

The first few chapters of this book present the basic information about WordPerfect that you must know in order to move on to more advanced functions. In these chapters you'll learn about the WordPerfect environment and the most important commands. Once you're familiar with how WordPerfect works and how to utilize some basic features, you'll be ready for the remaining chapters. In the last chapters of the book, you'll create actual documents step-by-step while learning how to use many of the same WordPerfect features you'd access during everyday work with the program.

Contents

1. Getting Started

In this chapter we'll present some background information about word processors and the operating system of your computer. Although we cannot discuss both of these topics in detail, this information should help you get started with WordPerfect. By knowing something about word processors and how the disk operating system works, you'll feel more comfortable learning WordPerfect. This is especially helpful if you don't have any experience using computers.

If you've never used a word processor before, you may not even be sure what a word processor is. So we'll explain what word processors are and the advantages of using them. If you have used a word processor before, you may find that some of WordPerfect's features are similar to another program's features.

1.1   What's a Word Processor?

In this section we'll briefly discuss what word processors are and how they differ from typewriters.

Even though word processors and typewriters can both produce printed documents, they have many differences. With a normal typewriter, text is entered directly onto the paper. But with a word processor, the text is first entered on the screen before it is printed.

One of the most important advantages of using a word processor is that, unlike a typewriter, word processors allow you to save text to disk. So, you can easily recall a saved document when needed. Because of this capability you can print more than one copy of a document. You could also reuse the same document several times by making a few minor changes.

Also, with a word processor you can edit and correct text on the screen before the document is printed. It's also possible to copy, delete and move certain text passages within a document.

As you already know, if you want to make these kinds of changes to a typewritten document, you usually have to type the entire document again.

For example, suppose that you have typed a letter to a friend telling him/her about your recent vacation. As you are reading the letter, you notice three spelling errors. You also realize that you forgot to tell your friend about the wonderful Italian restaurant you discovered during your travels.

Since you used a typewriter, there isn't an easy way to make the corrections. You could use correcting fluid on the misspelled words and then type over them. But it isn't possible to add a new paragraph to the middle of the letter.

With a word processor, however, these errors could easily be corrected. Since you can save any documents you create, you don't have to re-type an entire document in order to make a few corrections and additions. A misspelled word can simply be deleted and then replaced with the correct word. Also, a new paragraph can be inserted within the body of the letter.

In addition to making it easier to edit documents, word processors also offer special formatting capabilities, such as bold print, underlining and different font styles. These capabilities enable you to produce better-looking documents. Most word processors also provide a spell checking function that checks your document for misspelled words and then offers several possible replacements.

Word processors also contain many advanced features. For example, WordPerfect is capable of performing calculations within documents and merging information from several documents.

So, as you can see, there are many advantages to using a word processor instead of a typewriter. As we previously mentioned, WordPerfect is one of the best word processing programs currently on the market.

1.2   The Disk Operating System

The Disk Operating System, DOS, which is a vital part of your computer system, contains a group of programs that manage the many tasks that are needed in order to use your computer. These tasks include starting an application program, such as the WordPerfect word processor, preparing diskettes for storing data and locating data files on diskettes.

So, in order to use WordPerfect, you should have a basic understanding of DOS. Several of DOS' programs are moved from disk into the computer's memory or they are loaded when the computer is first switched on.

If you have a hard drive system, it can be configured to load DOS automatically when you switch on the computer. If you only have a floppy disk computer system, DOS must be loaded or booted from a diskette each time the computer is switched on.

Once DOS is loaded, you can communicate with your computer by entering commands. A command is an instruction telling the computer to perform a certain task.

Although you don't need extensive knowledge of DOS in order to use WordPerfect, there are several DOS commands that you should know how to use. This will make using WordPerfect easier. The following is a brief explanation of these commands:

CD
: Abbreviation for CHANGE DIRECTORY. This command determines the current directory. Unless a complete pathname is specified, a computer will search for files in this directory.

CHKDSK
: Abbreviation for CHECK DISK. This command provides various information, such as the total capacity and number of files, about the specified diskette. CHKDSK also indicates whether there are any errors on the diskette.

COPY
: With this command you can copy files. There are three ways to do this:

3

- Copy a file from one disk to another

- Copy a file to the same disk by using a different filename

- Copy a file from one drive to another and assign a new filename

DIR   Abbreviation for DIRECTORY. This command displays the directory of the disk in the current drive.

FORMAT   This command formats a disk. Formatting prepares the disk for storing data.

MD   Abbreviation for MAKE DIRECTORY. This command is used to create a directory.

When DOS is ready to accept your commands, it will display the *DOS prompt* on the screen. The prompt will look like one of the following: A:, B: or C:. The letter indicates which drive is in use. To change the drive, type the desired drive identifier, followed by a colon, and then press the [Enter] key:

  A:[Enter]

This DOS prompt indicates that you can either type a DOS command or start an application program, such as WordPerfect. To do this type the application's name at the prompt. For example, to start WordPerfect, enter:

  wp[Enter]

After you type a command or an application name, you may see the following message on your screen:

  Bad command or filename

If this happens, DOS is trying to tell you that either the command was entered incorrectly, or that the command or application program isn't on the disk that is currently being used. So, it is important that you carefully type in commands and application program names.

1.3   Creating Backups

When working with WordPerfect or any program, you should make backup copies of your data frequently. Making backup copies is important because data on a disk can be accidentally destroyed. You can back up entire disks by using the DOS command DISKCOPY, or back up specific files by using the COPY command.

Backing up an entire disk

To copy the contents of an entire disk, use the DISKCOPY command. For example, either of the following invokes DISKCOPY:

```
DISKCOPY A: A:
DISKCOPY
```

You will be prompted to insert a diskette into the drive. If you have two drives, insert the source diskette in drive A: and the target diskette in drive B:. The source diskette is the diskette you want copied and the target diskette is the diskette that will be the copy. The command is as follows:

```
DISKCOPY A: B:
```

Backing up files

To copy specific files, use the COPY command. There are a few methods you can use to copy files. You can copy a file from one disk to another. For example, if drive A: contains the source diskette and drive B: contains the target diskette, one of the following commands is used:

```
COPY FILENAME.EXT B:
COPY A:FILENAME.EXT B:
```

If you want to copy a file to the same disk by giving the copy a different filename than the original file, you would use the following command:

```
COPY OLDNAME.EXT NEWNAME.EXT
```

By doing this you'll have two identical files with different names on the same disk. It's also possible to copy a file from one drive to another and assign the file a new name. For example:

```
COPY A:OLDNAME.EXT B:NEWNAME.EXT
```

1.4   Starting WordPerfect

Obviously, before starting WordPerfect, you must install it on your hard drive if you have one. An installation program is included with your WordPerfect package. Before reading any further you should install WordPerfect using this program, which will take you through each step of the installation process.

Floppy disk drives   If you are working with two 720K (or higher) disk drives, start WordPerfect by first starting DOS and then inserting the WordPerfect 1 diskette in drive A:. Then, in drive B: insert the diskette on which you will store your files. Next, change the default drive to B: by entering:

    B:[Enter]

To start the program, enter:

    A:WP[Enter]

Then replace the WordPerfect 1 diskette with the WordPerfect 2 diskette.

Hard Drive   If you have a hard drive system, start DOS and then change to the directory that contains WP.EXE:

    CD \DIRNAME

Then enter WP and press [Enter]:

    WP[Enter]

2. The WordPerfect Environment

Now that you're ready to use WordPerfect, we'll begin by introducing you to the WordPerfect environment. You must first know how to use the basic elements of the program's environment. These elements include text entry, cursor movement and accessing menus and features. Once you're familiar with the WordPerfect environment, you'll be ready to learn about more advanced functions.

2.1 Entering Text

When you start WordPerfect you'll see the following screen:

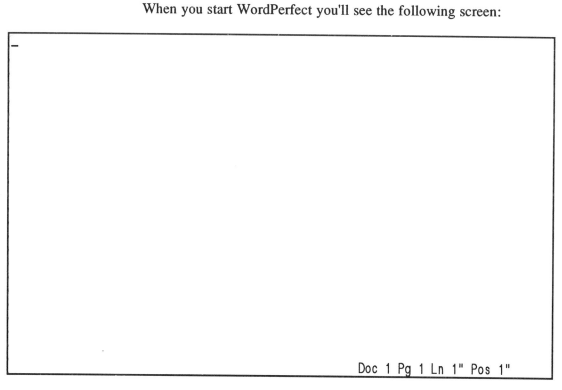

WordPerfect editing screen

This is the *editing screen*. A cursor will appear in the upper-left corner of the screen. At the bottom of the screen you'll see the *status line*. This line provides information about the document number, page number, line number and position of the cursor.

Let's enter some text. In the following examples we'll use the paragraph below:

```
With the WordPerfect word processor you can do more than simply type text. A word
processor also has many features that make it an indispensable tool for producing
all kinds of documents. For example, a word processor enables you to create and
edit text on the video display before it is printed. Because of this capability
you can quickly and easily make a variety of corrections.
```

Enter the first five words of the above paragraph:

```
With the WordPerfect word processor
```

Notice that the cursor position number changes in the status line. Now enter the rest of the paragraph. Do not press the (Enter) key until you reach the end of the paragraph.

Note: More text will fit on a line than is shown in our paragraph above.

Word wrapping   Notice that at the end of each line the text automatically continued on the next line without the (Enter) key being pressed. This process is called *word wrapping*. When a screen is filled with text, the cursor automatically moves to the left margin of the next line.

Note: WordPerfect uses the (Enter) key to end a paragraph or to send commands to the computer. Do not use this key to move the cursor unless you want to add a blank line to your document.

When you're finished you should see the following on your screen, don't worry if your screen differs slighty:

```
With the WordPerfect word processor you can do more than simply
type text. A word processor also has many features that make
it an indispensable tool for producing all kinds of documents. For
example, a word processor enables you to create and edit text on
the video display before it is printed. Because of this capability
you can quickly and easily make a variety of corrections.
_




                                          Doc 1 Pg 1 Ln 2.17" Pos 1"
```

WordPerfect screen with complete paragraph

2.2 Cursor Movement

To move the cursor within the text, use the four arrow keys. These keys are usually located on the right side of your keyboard. Each key either moves the cursor up, down, left or right, depending on the arrow displayed on the key.

Some keyboards also contain a separate group of number keys that are located on the right side of the keyboard. This is called the *numeric keypad*. These keys also contain the arrow keys.

The [Num Lock] key is used to control the function of these keys. When Num Lock is activated (the key is pressed and an indicator light is lit), the numbers can be used. When Num Lock isn't activated (the indicator light is off), the arrow keys can be used. If you're using a mouse, move the pointer to the desired location and click the mouse button.

Experiment with these keys now. Notice that each time you press a key the cursor moves up or down one letter. Also notice that the line number and position number in the status line changes as you use the arrow keys.

Use the [Ctrl] key and either the [→] or [←] key to move word by word in either direction. Try this now.

To move the cursor to the beginning of the line, press the [Home] key, then press the [←] key (don't press these keys simultaneously). To move to the end of a line, press the [End] key, or press [Home], then the [→] key. Try these keys now.

If you want to return to the top of the screen from anywhere in the document, press the [Home] key twice and then press the [↑] key. In order to move to the end of your document, press the [Home] key twice and then press the [↓] key.

Use the [Pg Up] key to move the cursor to the top of the previous page. The [Pg Dn] key will move the cursor to the top of the next page.

Notice how the status line changes accordingly while using these keys.

Here's a table showing basic cursor movement, to help you get through documents quickly. In this table, and throughout this book, you'll see two ways of notating keypresses:

- A plus sign between keys indicates that the first key should be pressed and held, then the second key should be pressed. Both keys should then be released. For example, [Ctrl]+[←] means that you should press and hold the [Ctrl] key, press the [←] key and release both keys immediately after pressing the [←] key.

- A comma between keys indicates that each key should be pressed and released in sequence. For example, [Home],[Home],[↑] means that you should press and release the [Home] key twice, then press and release the [↑] key.

Action	Key combination
One character left	[←]
One character right	[→]
One line down	[↓]
One line up	[↑]
One word left	[Ctrl]+[←]
One word right	[Ctrl]+[→]
Beginning of line	[Home][←]
End of line	[Home][→]
Beginning of document	[Home][Home][↑]
End of document	[Home][Home][↓]
Top of previous page	[Pg Up]
Top of next page	[Pg Dn]

2.3 Editing Text

The text you enter when creating a document will usually have to be edited. For example, you may want to add or delete words, or correct misspelled words. In WordPerfect the primary ways to edit text are through the Insert mode, the Typeover mode, the (Backspace) key and the (Del) key.

Insert mode

The Insert mode is the basic method of editing text in WordPerfect. This mode is automatically activated when you start WordPerfect. This mode will remain active unless you specifically change it. When you're in Insert mode, the text you enter is inserted at the current cursor position and any existing text moves to the right to accommodate the new text.

Let's return to our example paragraph. Suppose that you want to add the word "much" before "more" in the first line of the paragraph. To do this, move the cursor, either with the arrow keys or with the mouse, to the space directly before the "m" in "more". Now type a space by pressing the (Spacebar), which is the long key at the bottom of your keyboard. Then type the word "much". Your screen should look like the following:

```
With the WordPerfect word processor you can do much more than
simply type text. A word processor also has many features that make
it an indispensable tool for producing all kinds of documents. For
example, a word processor enables you to create and edit text on
the video display before it is printed. Because of this capability
you can quickly and easily make a variety of corrections.




















                                         Doc 1 Pg 1 Ln 1.83" Pos 7.5"
```

The word "much" has been added to our example paragraph

Typeover mode

When you use the Typeover mode, new text is typed over existing text. In order to activate this mode, press the (Ins) (Insert) key. When this key is pressed, the word Typeover will appear in the lower-left portion of your screen. Any text entered will replace any existing text in the current cursor location. To exit the Typeover mode and return to the Insert mode, press the (Ins) key again.

Now let's see how the Typeover mode works. This time, instead of adding a word, let's replace an existing word in the text. In our example paragraph, replace the word "type" in the first sentence with the word "enter". First move the cursor to the letter "t" in the word "type". Then press the (Ins) key; the word Typeover will appear on your screen. Now type the word "enter".

You should see the following on your screen:

```
┌─────────────────────────────────────────────────────────────────────────┐
│With the WordPerfect word processor you can do much more than              │
│simply entertext. A word processor also has many features that             │
│make it an indispensable tool for producing all kinds of documents.        │
│For example, a word processor enables you to create and edit text          │
│on the video display before it is printed. Because of this                 │
│capability you can quickly and easily make a variety of                    │
│corrections.                                                               │
│                                                                           │
│                                                                           │
│                                                                           │
│                                                                           │
│                                                                           │
│                                                                           │
│                                                                           │
│                                                                           │
│                                                                           │
│                                                                           │
│                                                                           │
│Typeover                                         Doc 1 Pg 1 Ln 2" Pos 3"   │
└─────────────────────────────────────────────────────────────────────────┘
```

The word "enter" has replaced the word "type" in our example paragraph

To disengage the Typeover mode, press the (Ins) key again and then press the (Spacebar) once to insert a space between "enter" and "text".

The (Backspace) and (Del) keys

In addition to the methods we just described, there are other ways to delete text from a document. The (Backspace) key and (Del) keys can also be used to delete text.

When you use the (Backspace) key you can delete characters to the left of the cursor. This key is usually located in the upper-right corner of the keyboard. The word "Backspace", the abbreviation "BkSp" or an arrow pointing left may appear on this key.

To demonstrate how the (Backspace) key works, erase the word "producing", which is located in the third line of our example text, and enter the word "creating". To do this, first move the cursor directly following the "g" in "producing". Then press the (Backspace) key until the word is erased. Now type the word "creating". Your example text should look something like the following:

```
With the WordPerfect word processor you can do much more than
simply enter text. A word processor also has many features that
make it an indispensable tool for creating all kinds of documents.
For example, a word processor enables you to create and edit text
on the video display before it is printed. Because of this
capability you can quickly and easily make a variety of
corrections.




















                                   Doc 1 Pg 1 Ln 2" Pos 3"
```

The word "producing" was deleted and "creating" was added to our example

The Del key deletes characters at the current cursor position. This key is usually located on the numeric keypad in the lower-right corner of the keyboard. The word "Delete" or the abbreviation "Del" will appear on this key. Make sure "Num Lock" is not active or this key will display a period when pressed. Press the Num Lock key to toggle "Num Lock" on or off.

Let's practice using this key by erasing the word "enables", which is located in the fourth line of our example text. We'll replace this word with "lets". First move the cursor to the "e" of "enables" and press the Del key until the word is erased. Then type the word "lets" in its place.

Now move the cursor to the word "to", in the same line, and press Del again until the word is erased. Your screen should now look something like the following:

With the WordPerfect word processor you can do much more than
simply enter text. A word processor also has many features that
make it an indispensable tool for creating all kinds of documents.
For example, a word processor lets you create and edit text on
the video display before it is printed. Because of this capability
you can quickly and easily make a variety of corrections.

Doc 1 Pg 1 Ln 1.83" Pos 7.5"

The word "lets" replaced the words "enables" and "to" in our example.

The following table lists those editing keys described in this section.

Key combination	Action
[Ins]	Toggle Typeover/Insert modes
[Backspace]	Delete characters to left of cursor
[Del]	Delete characters at current cursor position

2.4 Accessing Menus and Features

There are several ways to access WordPerfect's menus and features. They can be selected either with the keyboard by using the function keys, letter keys and number keys or with pull-down menus by using the arrow keys and (Enter), the number and letter keys, or by using a mouse.

In this book we'll provide instructions for using the pull-down menus, the keyboard and mouse for all of our examples. You should use whichever method is more comfortable for you. So, experiment with the different methods to determine which one you prefer. You may also feel comfortable using a combination of methods.

Function keys

Using the function keys is one way to access WordPerfect's various features. These keys, which are usually located at the top of the keyboard, are identified by the letter "F", followed by a number between 1 and 12. Each function key performs four tasks - one when the function key is pressed by itself and three others when the function key is pressed in conjunction with either the (Ctrl), (Alt) or (Shift) keys.

The WordPerfect package includes a template, which can be placed on your keyboard. This template indicates the feature corresponding to each function key. By using this template, you can quickly determine which key(s) you should press in order to activate a certain feature.

WordPerfect also supplies an on-screen template. To display this template, press the (F3) key twice. The following should appear on your screen:

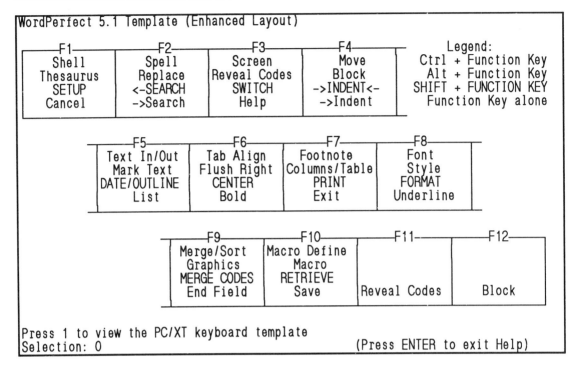

```
WordPerfect 5.1 Template (Enhanced Layout)
  ┌─F1──────────┬─F2──────────┬─F3──────────┬─F4──────────┐        Legend:
  │   Shell     │   Spell     │   Screen    │    Move     │   Ctrl + Function Key
  │ Thesaurus   │  Replace    │ Reveal Codes│   Block     │    Alt + Function Key
  │   SETUP     │ <-SEARCH    │   SWITCH    │ ->INDENT<-  │  SHIFT + FUNCTION KEY
  │   Cancel    │ ->Search    │    Help     │  ->Indent   │    Function Key alone
  └─────────────┴─────────────┴─────────────┴─────────────┘

      ┌─F5──────────┬─F6──────────┬─F7──────────┬─F8──────────┐
      │ Text In/Out │  Tab Align  │  Footnote   │    Font     │
      │  Mark Text  │ Flush Right │Columns/Table│   Style     │
      │ DATE/OUTLINE│   CENTER    │   PRINT     │  FORMAT     │
      │    List     │    Bold     │    Exit     │  Underline  │
      └─────────────┴─────────────┴─────────────┴─────────────┘

          ┌─F9──────────┬─F10─────────┬─F11─────────┬─F12─────────┐
          │ Merge/Sort  │Macro Define │             │             │
          │  Graphics   │   Macro     │             │             │
          │ MERGE CODES │  RETRIEVE   │             │             │
          │  End Field  │    Save     │Reveal Codes │   Block     │
          └─────────────┴─────────────┴─────────────┴─────────────┘

Press 1 to view the PC/XT keyboard template
Selection: 0                              (Press ENTER to exit Help)
```

WordPerfect's on-screen template

Pull-down menus

Another way to access WordPerfect's menus and features is with pull-down menus. To turn the pull-down menus on or off, either press ⟨Alt⟩+⟨=⟩ or, if you're using a mouse, press the right mouse button. The menu bar will appear at the top of your screen.

There are different ways to select the menus and activate the features. You can use the ⟨←⟩ and ⟨→⟩ keys to select a menu and then use the ⟨↑⟩ and ⟨↓⟩ keys to select a feature. Activate the selected feature by pressing ⟨Enter⟩.

Let's try selecting a menu with this method. First turn on the pull-down menus by pressing ⟨Alt⟩+⟨=⟩ or pressing the right mouse button.

```
File Edit Search Layout Mark Tools Font Graphics Help        (Press F3 for Help)
simply enter text. A word processor also has many features that
make it an indispensable tool for creating all kinds of documents.
For example, a word processor lets you create and edit text on
the video display before it is printed. Because of this capability
you can quickly and easily make a variety of corrections.




                                            Doc 1 Pg 1 Ln 1.83" Pos 7.5"
```

The pull-down menu bar

Press the →] key until you reach the Help menu. Notice that as you press this key, the selected menu appears in reverse video (foreground and background colors change). Now press the ↓] key. The Help menu's features will appear under the menu title.

```
┌────────────────────────────────────────────┬──────────────┬─────────────┐
│File Edit Search Layout Mark Tools Font Graphics He│lp           │(Press F3 for Help)│
│simply enter text. A word processor also has many│ Help         │at           │
│make it an indispensable tool for creating all ki│ Index        │ents.        │
│For example, a word processor lets you create and│ Template     │n the        │
│video display before it is printed. Because of th└──────────────┘y you        │
│can quickly and easily make a variety of corrections.                       │
│                                                                            │
│                                                                            │
│                                                                            │
│                                                                            │
│                                                                            │
│                                                                            │
│                                                                            │
│                                                                            │
│                                                                            │
│                                                                            │
│                                                                            │
│                                                                            │
│                                        Doc 1 Pg 1 Ln 1.83" Pos 6.4"        │
└────────────────────────────────────────────────────────────────────────┘
```

The Help menu activated

To select a feature, continue to press the ⬇ key until the desired feature is displayed in reverse video and press (Enter). For example, press the ⬇ key until the Template feature is selected and then press (Enter). The WordPerfect template will appear on your screen. Now exit the template by pressing (Enter) and activate the pull-down menus again.

If you look at the pull-down menus on the menu bar, you'll notice that one letter in each menu title is highlighted (appears different from the rest of the letters). Another way to select menus and features is to press the letter key that corresponds to the highlighted letter in the menu title or feature name.

Now let's use this method to activate the Help menu. Press the (H) key to activate this menu; Help's features appear under the menu title. To activate the Index feature, press the (I) key. A listing of help topics will appear on the screen. To exit this feature, press (Enter). Then activate the pull-down menus again.

It's also possible to select and activate menus and features by using a mouse. Click (press and release) the right mouse button to invoke the menu. Move the mouse pointer to the appropriate menu title and press the left mouse button. While holding down the mouse button, drag the mouse pointer to the appropriate feature and release the mouse button.

Note: If you accidentally select the incorrect menu, you can return to the normal menu bar by pressing the (Esc) key.

Menu options   After activating certain WordPerfect features either with the function keys or the pull-down menus, an additional menu will appear. These menus contain additional options that can be selected. For example, let's activate the Document feature from the Layout menu. To do this, either press (Shift)+(F8) and then press (3) or activate the pull-down menu ((Alt)+(=) or click with the mouse), select the Layout menu and activate the Document feature. The following will appear on the screen:

```
Format: Document

   1 - Display Pitch - Automatic Yes
                      Width     0.1"

   2 - Initial Codes

   3 - Initial Base Font        Courier 10 Pitch

   4 - Redline Method           Printer Dependent

   5 - Summary




Selection: 0
```

Format Document menu

There are various ways you can select an option from these menus. You can either type the option number that appears to the left of the option, press the letter key that corresponds to the highlighted letter in the option or, if you're using a mouse, move the mouse pointer to the appropriate option and click the mouse button.

We'll discuss menu options in more detail later in this book. To exit this menu, press F7. This will return you to the normal editing screen.

The following table lists the feature access keys described in this section.

Key combination	Action
Alt + =	Activate pull-down menu
F3	Help
F3 , F3	Template
F7	Exit

The following table lists the features described in this section, as accessed from menus.

Menu selection	Action
Right mouse button	Activate pull-down menu
Help/Help	Help
Help/Template	Template
File/Exit	Exit

2.5 Invisible Codes

The normal editing screen of WordPerfect only displays the text of your document. Any features that are used to change the appearance of the text aren't displayed. Instead, codes are used to instruct the computer and printer to perform tasks. These codes are actually hidden commands that are inserted into your document.

There are two kinds of codes: *Paired codes* and *open codes.*

Paired codes   These codes indicate attributes, such as bold, italics and underlining, and work in pairs (one code enables the attribute, while a second code disables the attribute).

This type of code is used when you will be switching an attribute on and off.

Open codes   These codes affect the document from the point they are inserted to the end of the document. So these codes aren't switched off.

Open codes are usually used to establish formatting settings that should be used throughout your document, such as margin settings.

To display the invisible codes in a document, press the [Alt]+[F3] keys, or select Reveal Codes from the Edit menu using the pull-down menus or the mouse. This activates the Reveal Codes feature.

Your screen will be divided into two sections, which are separated by a tab ruler. The lower section displays the text of the normal editing screen and the codes that were selected for this text. The triangles in the tab ruler represent tabs.

Notice that the cursor is located within the same place in both sections. However, in the normal editing screen, the cursor appears as a blinking dash. But in the lower section the cursor appears as a rectangle, which highlights the character on which it's located.

Note: We'll explain codes in more detail later in this book.

23

To return to the normal editing screen, press ⌨Alt⌨+⌨F3⌨ again, or select Reveal Codes from the Edit menu using the keyboard or the mouse.

Now you should be more familiar with the WordPerfect environment and feel more comfortable using the program. In this chapter you've learned how to enter and move the cursor around the screen. You've also learned how to use the keys that help you edit text and the keys that enable you to access WordPerfect's features.

3. Basic Features

After looking at the on-screen template in Chapter 2, you may be feeling overwhelmed by WordPerfect because it contains so many commands. This is nothing to be concerned about—you may never use most of the commands. Since this is a book intended for beginners, we're going to focus on the basic commands you'll need to control WordPerfect.

Almost every word processing program in existence contain a few basic commands that are the most frequently used. These commands enable you to save and retrieve text, cancel certain actions, exit a document or the program and obtain help about the program. In WordPerfect, the Save, Exit, Retrieve, Cancel and Help features perform these tasks.

Once you've learned how to use these features, you'll be on your way to mastering the more advanced features WordPerfect offers. Also, once you're familiar with these basic features, you'll have the power to begin creating documents immediately. So, you can practice what you've learned without worrying about all of the other WordPerfect features.

In this chapter we'll discuss the Save, Exit, Retrieve, Cancel and Help features in detail. Also, as in the previous chapter, you can practice what you learn by using the provided examples.

3.1 Saving Text

In WordPerfect, you can save text with or without exiting the program. With the Save feature you can save your document without exiting WordPerfect and without losing your place in your document.

It's important to save your document occasionally so that you don't lose any of your changes if your computer crashes or if a power failure occurs. Remember that the only way to store your document permanently is to save it.

Fast Save

How fast a document is saved depends on whether the Fast Save option, in the Setup Environment menu, is active. If this option is set to Yes, which is the default setting, WordPerfect saves the document faster than if this option is set to No. This is faster because WordPerfect doesn't format the document for printing when the document is saved. So when a document that has been fast saved from disk is printed, WordPerfect retrieves the document and, in the background, checks the formatting before printing. If the Fast Save option is set to No, WordPerfect will completely format the document when it is saved.

To change this setting, select Setup either by pressing (Shift)+(F1) and selecting Environment from the Setup menu by pressing (3) or (E) or by activating the menu bar and selecting the Setup feature from the File menu and activating Environment. Select Fast Save by pressing (5). Then either press (Y) or (N) to switch this option on or off. To return to the normal editing screen, press Exit ((F7)).

Using Save

Now let's save the text we've entered in the previous examples. First activate the Save feature by pressing (F10) or by selecting Save from the File menu either with the keyboard or by using a mouse. The line Document to be saved: will appear in the lower-left corner of the screen:

```
With the WordPerfect word processor you can do much more than
simply enter text. A word processor also has many features that
make it an indispensable tool for creating all kinds of documents.
For example, a word processor lets you create and edit text on the
video display before it is printed. Because of this capability you
can quickly and easily make a variety of corrections.




















Document to be saved:
```

Activating the Save feature

Filenames

Now you must enter a filename for the document. WordPerfect saves files according to MS-DOS conventions. This means that a filename can only have a maximum of 8 characters and, if desired, an extension of no more than 3 characters.

Note:

WordPerfect 5.1 does allow you to use a filename that is longer than 8 characters. By using the Long Document Names option in the Document Management/Summary submenu of Setup/Environment, you can enter a document name that contains a maximum of 68 characters. If this option is set to Yes, when you save a document you'll be asked to enter a long document name, document type and a DOS filename. For more information consult your WordPerfect manual.

Unless you specify a full pathname, which includes the drive letter and subdirectory names, a document is saved in the default directory. When WordPerfect is started, this is the directory that is selected for saving and retrieving files.

Now let's determine the default directory. First press [Esc] or Cancel ([F1]) to return to the normal editing screen. Then press [F5] or activate the List Files feature from the File menu by using the keyboard or the mouse.

The default directory will appear in the lower-left corner of the screen. It should look similar to the following:

```
With the WordPerfect word processor you can do much more than
simply enter text. A word processor also has many features that
make it an indispensable tool for creating all kinds of documents.
For example, a word processor lets you create and edit text on the
video display before it is printed. Because of this capability you
can quickly and easily make a variety of corrections.




















Dir C:\*.*                                (Type = to change default Dir)
```

Determining the default directory

To return to the normal editing screen, press Cancel ([F1]).

If you want to save a file in a directory other than the default directory, you must use a pathname. However, remember that in order to retrieve a document that isn't in the default directory, you must enter the entire pathname.

For our example text, we'll use the default directory. So activate Save again by pressing [F10] or by selecting Save from the File menu either with the keyboard or with a mouse. Now type PRACTICE and press [Enter].

28

WordPerfect saves the document in the default directory and displays the document name in the status line. Your screen should look similar to the following:

```
With the WordPerfect word processor you can do much more than
simply enter text. A word processor also has many features that
make it an indispensable tool for creating all kinds of documents.
For example, a word processor lets you create and edit text on the
video display before it is printed. Because of this capability you
can quickly and easily make a variety of corrections.




















C:\PRACTICE                                Doc 1 Pg 1 Ln 1.83" Pos 6.4"
```

Document name displayed in the status line

3.2 Exiting

WordPerfect's Exit feature does more than enable you to leave a document or the WordPerfect program. As we'll explain in this section, this feature can be used in several ways.

Exiting a document and WordPerfect

If you want to leave a document that's in the normal editing screen, press ⌐F 7⌐ or select Exit from the File menu (press ⌐Alt⌐+⌐=⌐ or press the right mouse button to activate the menu bar) with either the keyboard or a mouse. Try this now. The following should appear on your screen:

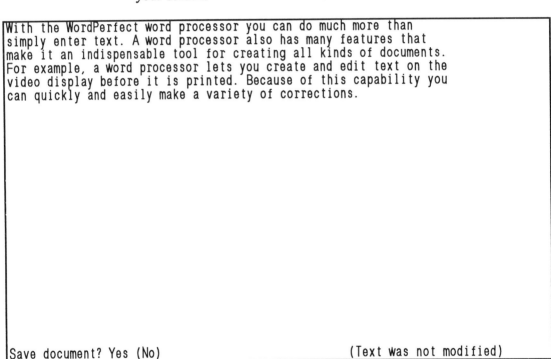

```
With the WordPerfect word processor you can do much more than
simply enter text. A word processor also has many features that
make it an indispensable tool for creating all kinds of documents.
For example, a word processor lets you create and edit text on the
video display before it is printed. Because of this capability you
can quickly and easily make a variety of corrections.




















Save document? Yes (No)                          (Text was not modified)
```

Activating the Exit feature

WordPerfect asks whether or not you want to save the document. Notice the Text was not modified message in the lower-right corner of the screen in the above figure. This message will appear when no changes were made to the document. If this message doesn't appear, the document was changed in some way. Press ⌐N⌐ to answer this prompt if you haven't made any changes to the document or you don't want to save the changes you've made.

The following will appear on your screen:

```
With the WordPerfect word processor you can do much more than
simply enter text. A word processor also has many features that
make it an indispensable tool for creating all kinds of documents.
For example, a word processor lets you create and edit text on the
video display before it is printed. Because of this capability you
can quickly and easily make a variety of corrections.




















Exit WP? No (Yes)                              (Cancel to return to document)
```

The Exit WP prompt

Either press Ⓨ to leave the WordPerfect program and return to DOS or press Ⓝ clear the screen and begin a new document.

To save the document on the screen before exiting, press Ⓨ. Depending on whether or not the document was previously saved, different messages will appear on the screen. For our example, press Ⓨ now.

If this is the first time the document has been saved, WordPerfect asks for a filename. Enter an appropriate filename (see "Filenames" in the previous section) and press [Enter]. The Exit WP? prompt, as shown above, will appear.

If the document was saved at another time, the document's filename will appear in the status line. Since you saved the example document

31

in the previous section, the filename PRACTICE should appear in the status line. You can either replace the existing file with the file on the screen or enter a new filename. To replace the existing file, press [Enter]. Although you haven't changed your document, press [Enter] so that you can see how Exit works. WordPerfect will ask whether the existing file should be replaced with the current version.

```
With the WordPerfect word processor you can do much more than
simply enter text. A word processor also has many features that
make it an indispensable tool for creating all kinds of documents.
For example, a word processor lets you create and edit text on the
video display before it is printed. Because of this capability you
can quickly and easily make a variety of corrections.




















Replace C:\PRACTICE? No (Yes)
```

Replace existing document prompt

If you press [Y] (Yes) or [Enter], the existing file will be replaced with the file on the screen. Press [Enter] to save the file. If you press [N] (No), WordPerfect will ask you to enter a new filename. Doing this enables you to retain both the new and old versions of a file.

There are different ways to enter a different filename for the file. If the new filename will be completely different from the old filename simply press any letter key. Doing this deletes the name in the Document to be saved: prompt so that you can enter the new name. However, you can also edit the existing name. To do this press the [→] or [←] keys to move to the location where you want to delete or add a letter. Use the [Backspace] and [Del] keys to delete characters. When the new filename is entered, press the [Enter] key. Then

WordPerfect asks if you want to exit the program. Press [N] to clear the screen but stay in WordPerfect.

Note: If you decide you don't want to exit or save a document during any of these steps, you press Cancel ([F1]) at the Save or Exit prompts. We'll discuss the Cancel feature later in this chapter.

Exiting options and menus   The Exit feature can also be used to leave menus and submenus so that you can return to a previous menu or the current document. Let's try doing this now. Activate the Format Page submenu. To do this using the function keys, press [Shift]+[F8]. The main Format menu will appear. Press [2] or [P] or click with the mouse to activate the Page option. To use the pull-down menus, press [Alt]+[=] or press the right mouse button to activate the menu bar and select Page from the Layout menu with the keyboard or with the mouse. The following submenu should appear on the screen:

```
Format: Page

    1 - Center Page (top to bottom)     No

    2 - Force Odd/Even Page

    3 - Headers

    4 - Footers

    5 - Margins - Top                    1"
                  Bottom                 1"

    6 - Page Numbering

    7 - Paper Size                       8.5" x 11"
                  Type                   Standard

    8 - Suppress (this page only)




Selection: 0
```

The Format Page submenu

Now press 1 or C or use the mouse to select the Center Page (top to bottom) option. Notice that the cursor is now located at this option. Suppose that you wanted to activate a different option instead of this one. Simply press F7 to leave the option. The cursor will now return to the Selection: line at the bottom of the screen and the option's setting will remain the same. Now press 6 or N or use the mouse to activate the Page Numbering option. The Format Page Numbering submenu should appear on your screen:

```
Format: Page Numbering

    1 - New Page Number        1

    2 - Page Number Style      ^B

    3 - Insert Page Number

    4 - Page Number Position No page numbering












Selection: 0
```

The Format Page submenu

Suppose that you wanted to leave this menu and return to your document. To do this, press F7.

Although Exit can be used to exit options and menus, remember that any settings that were made are automatically saved when you press F7. So, if you want to cancel a setting that you've made, use Cancel (F1) instead of Exit. We'll discuss Cancel later in this chapter. The Exit feature can also be used to switch between two documents. We'll discuss this in more detail in Section 4.4.

3.3   Retrieving Files

In this section we'll retrieve or load the document we exited in the previous section. As you'll see, it's easy to retrieve documents in WordPerfect. However, depending on the situation, different steps must be performed.

When you saved your sample document, PRACTICE, in the Save section earlier in this chapter, the document was saved as a file on the hard drive. In WordPerfect, documents are always saved as files on either the hard drive or floppy diskettes. In order to use an existing document, you must retrieve a copy of the file from the storage medium on which it was saved—either the hard drive or a diskette.

Once a file is loaded, you can edit it or print it using a printer. However, remember that the document that appears on your screen is only a copy of the file you retrieved. So if you make any changes to the document, you must use Save or Exit to save these changes. If you don't save your changes, the document will be the same as the most recently retrieved version of the file.

Using Retrieve   One way to retrieve files is with the Retrieve feature. Use this feature when you know the filename of the document you want to retrieve. Activate Retrieve by pressing (Shift)+(F10) or by selecting Retrieve from the File menu by activating the menu bar ((Alt)+(=) or pressing the right mouse button) and then using the keyboard or the mouse. You should see the following on your screen:

```
Document to be retrieved:                                    (List Files)
```

Activating Retrieve

You are prompted to enter the name of the document you want to retrieve. Let's retrieve our sample document PRACTICE. To do this, type PRACTICE and press ⌈Enter⌉. The document should appear on the screen.

Correcting
filenames

If you typed the filename incorrectly, or the file wasn't saved, the following error message will appear instead of the document:

```
Error: File Not Found
```

When this happens, WordPerfect will display the Document to be retrieved: prompt again and the incorrect filename. For example, if you typed PRRCTICE instead of PRACTICE, the following would appear after the File Not Found error message:

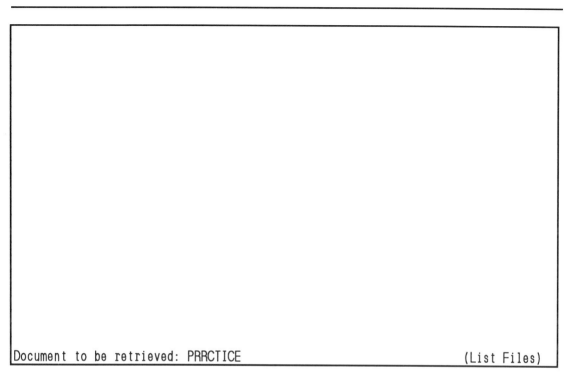

Document to be retrieved: PRRCTICE	(List Files)

Incorrect filename

Instead of retyping the entire filename, you can edit the one displayed on the screen. To correct the filename, use the arrow keys and the [Backspace] and [Del] keys. Once the correct filename appears on the screen, you can press [Enter] to retrieve the file.

Determining the current directory

Since you are located in the same directory in which the PRACTICE document is saved, you were able to retrieve the document by entering only its filename. However, you can only do this when you're already located in the directory in which the file is located. To retrieve a document in a different directory, you must enter the document's complete pathname.

If you don't know in which directory you're currently located, there is an easy way to determine this. The List ([F5]) feature displays, in the status line, the name of the default directory. Let's use this feature now. Activate List by pressing the [F5] key or by activating the pull-down menus ([Alt]+[=] or press the right mouse button) and selecting List Files from the File menu either with the keyboard or mouse. Your screen should look similar to the following:

37

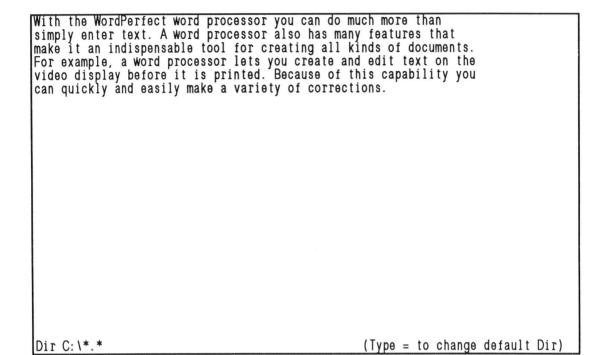

With the WordPerfect word processor you can do much more than
simply enter text. A word processor also has many features that
make it an indispensable tool for creating all kinds of documents.
For example, a word processor lets you create and edit text on the
video display before it is printed. Because of this capability you
can quickly and easily make a variety of corrections.

Dir C:*.*   (Type = to change default Dir)

The List feature activated

To return to the normal editing screen press Cancel (F1). There is
another way you can retrieve a document. Before discussing this, first
exit the Practice document. To do this, press F7 or select Exit from
the File menu. Then press N twice to clear the screen.

Using List

It's also possible to retrieve files using the List feature. You should
use this feature when you don't know the filename of the document
you want to retrieve but you do know the directory in which the file
is located.

Now try using List to retrieve our sample document, Practice.
Activate List again by pressing F5 or using the pull-down menus
and the keyboard or mouse. The default directory appears in the
status line. To display the files of this directory, simply press Enter.
A display similar to the following should appear on the screen:

```
┌──────────────────────────────────────────────────────────────────────────┐
│05-26-91  06:14p              Directory C:\*.*                              │
│Document size:      909   Free:  1,847,296 Used:      69,810    Files:     7 │
│                                                                            │
│  .   Current   <Dir>                   ..   Parent    <Dir>                │
│DOS      .      <Dir>  09-21-90 08:40a  EXCEL3   .      <Dir>  01-30-91 08:55p│
│HIJAAK1 .       <Dir>  05-16-91 08:37a  HSG      .      <Dir>  05-16-91 08:37a│
│MYM      .      <Dir>  05-15-91 05:04p  MYM7     .      <Dir>  05-15-91 04:26p│
│PCTOOLS6.       <Dir>  01-30-91 08:15p  SCREENS  .      <Dir>  05-16-91 09:09a│
│TEMP02  .       <Dir>  05-10-91 09:31p  TEMP03   .      <Dir>  01-30-91 07:33p│
│TEMP04  .       <Dir>  01-30-91 07:32p  TEMP05   .      <Dir>  01-30-91 07:31p│
│WINDOWS .       <Dir>  12-04-90 10:44p  WINWORD  .      <Dir>  12-15-90 04:18p│
│WP_DOC  .       <Dir>  05-16-91 08:50a  WP51     .      <Dir>  05-16-91 08:38a│
│AUTOEXEC.BAT      203  05-16-91 08:56a  COMMAND  .COM  47,845  04-09-91 05:00a│
│CONFIG  .SYS      253  05-10-91 10:38p  MOUSE    .SYS  11,153  06-17-86 03:05p│
│PRACTICE.         959  05-26-91 05:37p  QBASIC   .INI      48  12-20-90 09:16a│
│WINA20  .386    9,349  04-09-91 05:00a                                      │
│                                                                            │
│                                                                            │
│                                                                            │
│                                                                            │
│                                                                            │
│                                                                            │
│1 Retrieve; 2 Delete; 3 Move/Rename; 4 Print; 5 Short/Long Display;         │
│6 Look; 7 Other Directory; 8 Copy; 9 Find; N Name Search: 6                 │
└──────────────────────────────────────────────────────────────────────────┘
```

Displaying the files of the default directory

You should see the filename PRACTICE in the list of files. Suppose that you're not sure whether this is the file you want to retrieve. The Look option from the File List menu at the bottom of the screen enables you to display a file without retrieving it. To do this, use the arrow keys to move the cursor to the filename PRACTICE and press ⑥ or [Enter] to activate Look. The following should appear on your screen:

```
┌─────────────────────────────────────────────────────────────────────┐
│File: C:\PRACTICE                    WP5.1      Revised: 06-03-91 10:24p│
│                                                                       │
│With the WordPerfect word processor you can do much more than          │
│simply enter text. A word processor also has many features that        │
│make it an indispensable tool for creating all kinds of documents.     │
│For example, a word processor lets you create and edit text on the     │
│video display before it is printed. Because of this capability you     │
│can quickly and easily make a variety of corrections.                  │
│                                                                       │
│                                                                       │
│                                                                       │
│                                                                       │
│                                                                       │
│                                                                       │
│                                                                       │
│                                                                       │
│                                                                       │
│                                                                       │
│                                                                       │
│Look: 1 Next Doc; 2 Prev Doc: 0                                        │
└─────────────────────────────────────────────────────────────────────┘
```

Displaying a file with the Look option

Once you've determined whether or not you want to retrieve the document, you can either activate the Next Document option (⬚1⬚) to display the next file in the File List screen or the Previous Document option (⬚2⬚) to display the file listed before the one that is currently displayed in the Look screen. Otherwise you can return to the List Files screen by pressing Exit (⬚F7⬚) or the ⬚Spacebar⬚.

Now to retrieve this file, use the arrow keys to move to the filename and then activate the Retrieve option by pressing ⬚1⬚ or ⬚R⬚. The document should appear on the screen.

To retrieve a file that is located in a directory other than the default directory, simply activate List as we explained above and enter the name of the appropriate directory. Then press ⬚Enter⬚. The files of the specified directory will be displayed on the screen. Move the cursor to the appropriate filename and press ⬚1⬚ or ⬚R⬚.

3.4 Cancel

When you're first learning how to use a new program it's reassuring to know that if you make a mistake or change your mind, you can easily cancel your actions. In WordPerfect you can use the Cancel feature (F1) to exit menus, options and prompts without saving any changes that were made. Cancel can also be used to take you one level back when you're using the pull-down menus.

Menus and prompts

If you want to leave a menu, option or prompt and return to the previous level, simply press F1. Depending on the option or the menu, doing this will either take you to another menu or back to the normal editing screen.

Now let's try using Cancel. Activate the Print feature either by pressing Shift+F7 or by activating the menu bar (Alt+= or press the right mouse button) and selecting Print from the File menu with the keyboard or mouse. The following should appear on your screen:

```
┌─────────────────────────────────────────────────────────────────────────┐
│Print                                                                      │
│       1 - Full Document                                                   │
│       2 - Page                                                            │
│       3 - Document on Disk                                                │
│       4 - Control Printer                                                 │
│       5 - Multiple Pages                                                  │
│       6 - View Document                                                   │
│       7 - Initialize Printer                                              │
│                                                                           │
│                                                                           │
│Options                                                                    │
│                                                                           │
│       S - Select Printer                                                  │
│       B - Binding Offset                  0"                              │
│       N - Number of Copies                1                              │
│       U - Multiple Copies Generated by    WordPerfect                     │
│       G - Graphics Quality                Medium                          │
│       T - Text Quality                    High                            │
│                                                                           │
│                                                                           │
│                                                                           │
│                                                                           │
│Selection: 0                                                               │
└─────────────────────────────────────────────────────────────────────────┘
```

Activating the Print menu

Now press Cancel (F1). You will be returned to the normal editing screen. If you made any changes to the Print menu settings, they would not be saved. So, if you wanted to exit a menu or option and save any changes that were made, you should use the Exit feature instead of Cancel.

Note:

Cancel cannot be used to leave the Help feature. If you press F1 while in Help, the help screen for Cancel will be displayed. Only Enter and Spacebar can be used to leave Help.

As we mentioned, you can also use Cancel to exit prompts that appear in the status line. For example, activate the Save feature by pressing F10 or by selecting Save from the File menu. The Document to be saved: prompt will appear in the status line. Now press F1. The prompt disappears and you are returned to the normal editing screen.

Pull-down menus   When you're using the pull-down menus and want to return to the
previous level, you can press either Cancel (F1) or the Esc key.
For example, let's select Document from the Layout menu. To do
this, activate the menu bar by pressing Alt+= or by pressing the
right mouse button and then select Document from the Layout menu
with either the keyboard or the mouse. The Format Document
submenu appears. Now press F1 (or Esc). Since Cancel takes you
one level back, the Format menu will appear on the screen.

```
Format

    1 - Line
                Hyphenation                 Line Spacing
                Justification               Margins Left/Right
                Line Height                 Tab Set
                Line Numbering              Widow/Orphan Protection

    2 - Page
                Center Page (top to bottom) Page Numbering
                Force Odd/Even Page         Paper Size/Type
                Headers and Footers         Suppress
                Margins Top/Bottom

    3 - Document
                Display Pitch               Redline Method
                Initial Codes/Font          Summary

    4 - Other
                Advance                     Overstrike
                Conditional End of Page     Printer Functions
                Decimal Characters          Underline Spaces/Tabs
                Language                    Border Options

Selection: 0
```

The Format menu

Now press F1 (or Esc) again. You will be returned to the normal
editing screen. If you want to return directly to the normal editing
screen from a menu or submenu, you should press Exit (F7).

Using the mouse   If you're using a mouse, you can exit menus, options and prompts without using Cancel. To exit menus and options, click the middle button on a three button mouse and on a two button mouse hold one button down and click the other. To move one level back when using the pull-down menus, simply click the center button on a three button mouse and press one button and click the other on a two button mouse. To exit the pull-down menus completely, press the right mouse button on either type of mouse.

Cancel also has some other important uses, such as recovering deleted text and stopping a search operation or a macro operation. We'll discuss these uses later in this book.

3.5   Help

WordPerfect's Help feature (F3) provides information, on your screen, about various WordPerfect features and options. So you can access the information you need, while working in WordPerfect, without referring to your manual. Since there are several ways to access the various information Help provides, this feature is a very useful and flexible tool. In this section we'll discuss all of the ways you can use Help.

Activating Help from the normal editing screen

When Help is activated from the normal editing screen, the main Help menu will appear. Let's activate Help now by pressing the F3 key or by activating the menu bar (Alt+= or press the right mouse button) and selecting Help from the Help menu with the keyboard or the mouse. The following should appear on your screen:

```
┌─────────────────────────────────────────────────────────────────────┐
│Help                                        WP 5.1    06/29/90         │
│                                                                       │
│                                                                       │
│   Press any letter to get an alphabetical list of features.           │
│                                                                       │
│      The list will include the features that start with that letter,  │
│      along with the name of the key where the feature is found.  You  │
│      can then press that key to get a description of how the feature  │
│      works.                                                           │
│                                                                       │
│                                                                       │
│   Press any function key to get information about the use of the key.  │
│                                                                       │
│      Some keys may let you choose from a menu to get more information  │
│      about various options.  Press HELP again to display the template. │
│                                                                       │
│                                                                       │
│                                                                       │
│                                                                       │
│                                                                       │
│                                                                       │
│Selection: 0                            (Press ENTER to exit Help)     │
└─────────────────────────────────────────────────────────────────────┘
```

The main Help screen

This menu contains instructions on how to use Help. From this menu you can display an alphabetical list of features by pressing any letter key. The list will contain features that start with the specified letter. For example, suppose that you need information on how to change character spacing but you don't know which feature you would use to do this. Press the Ⓒ key to display information about character spacing. You should see the following on your screen:

```
┌─────────────────────────────────────────────────────────────────────────┐
│Features [C]                      WordPerfect Key   Keystrokes             │
│                                                                           │
│Cancel                            Cancel            F1                     │
│Cancel Hyphenation Code           Home              Home,/                 │
│Cancel Print Job(s)               Print             Shft-F7,4,1            │
│Capitalize Block (Block On)       Switch            Shft-F3,1              │
│Cartridges and Fonts              Print             Shft-F7,s,3,4          │
│Case Conversion (Block On)        Switch            Shft-F3               │
│Center Block (Block On)           Center            Shft-F6               │
│Center Justification              Format            Shft-F8,1,3,2          │
│Center Page (Top to Bottom)       Format            Shft-F8,2,1            │
│Center Tab Setting                Format            Shft-F8,1,8,c          │
│Center Text                       Center            Shft-F6               │
│Centered Text With Dot Leaders    Center            Shft-F6,Shft-F6        │
│Centimeters, Units of Measure     Setup             Shft-F1,3,8            │
│Change Comment to Text            Text In/Out       Ctrl-F5,4,3            │
│Change Default Directory          List              F5,=,Dir name,Enter    │
│Change Font                       Font              Ctrl-F8               │
│Change Supplementary Dictionary   Spell             Ctrl-F2,4              │
│Change Text to Comment (Block On) Text In/Out       Shft-F5               │
│Character Sets                    Compose           Ctrl-v or Ctrl-2       │
│Character Spacing                 Format            Shft-F8,4,6,3          │
│More... Press c to continue.                                               │
│                                                                           │
│Selection: 0                                        (Press ENTER to exit Help)│
└─────────────────────────────────────────────────────────────────────────┘
```

Activating the list of features

Note:

It's also possible to access the alphabetical list of features automatically without first displaying the main Help menu. To do this, activate the menu bar ([Alt]+[=] or press the right mouse button) and then select Index from the Help menu with the keyboard or with the mouse. The first screen of the features list will appear (starting with the letter "A"). To access other features, simply press the appropriate letter key.

As you can see, the features beginning with the letter "C" are displayed on the screen. The appropriate WordPerfect keystroke name and keystroke appear next to each feature. So, you must use the Format feature in order to set the character spacing option, which can be activated by pressing [Shift]+[F8], [4],[6],[3].

Note: If there are more entries for a specific letter than can fit on one screen page, a message will appear at the bottom of the list. For example, in the previous figure, the message "More...Press c to continue." appears. Simply press the indicated letter until the desired feature appears. To return to the first screen, continue to press the same letter key.

If, after you activate a list of features and determine the appropriate keystroke to use, you're still not sure how to use a feature, Help provides additional information. To access more information about a feature, press the appropriate keystroke for the feature. For example, for information on how to set character spacing, press the (Shift)+(F 8), (4),(6),(3) keys. Press (F 3). The following should appear on your screen:

```
┌─────────────────────────────────────────────────────────────────────────┐
│Word/Letter Spacing                                                        │
│                                                                           │
│    Adjusts spacing between adjacent words and letters. There are four     │
│    settings:                                                              │
│                                                                           │
│    Normal - Uses the spacing which was set by the printer manufacturer    │
│                                                                           │
│    Optimal - Uses the spacing that looks best according to WordPerfect    │
│                                                                           │
│    Percent of Optimal - Lets you enter a width of your own. The setting you│
│         enter is a percentage of the Optimal setting. 100% is exactly like│
│         choosing Optimal                                                  │
│                                                                           │
│    Set Pitch - Allows you to enter a pitch.                               │
│                                                                           │
│                                                                           │
│                                                                           │
│                                                                           │
│                                                                           │
│                                                                           │
│                                                                           │
│Selection: 0                                     (Press ENTER to exit Help)│
└─────────────────────────────────────────────────────────────────────────┘
```

Accessing information about the character spacing feature

This screen provides information on how to set the word or letter spacing. Now you can either exit Help by pressing (Enter) or continue to look up information. You don't have to leave this screen to access information about other features. For example, suppose that you need some information about the Search feature. If you don't know the keystroke for this feature, you could press Ⓢ from the current screen to display features that begin with the letter "S" and then press the keystroke that is displayed. However, if you already know the keystroke for the feature you could press the appropriate keys from the current screen to display a description of the feature. Let's try this now; press 〔F2〕. The following should appear on your screen:

```
Search

   Searches forward (F2) or backward (Shift-F2) through your text for a
   specific combination of characters and/or codes.  After entering the
   search text, press Search again to start the search.  If the text is
   found, the cursor will be positioned just after (to the right of) it.
   Lowercase letters in the search text match both lowercase and uppercase.
   Uppercase letters match only uppercase.

   Extended Search
   Pressing Home before pressing Search extends the search into headers,
   footers, footnotes, endnotes, graphics box captions, and text boxes.  To
   continue the extended search, press Home, Search.




Selection: 0                              (Press ENTER to exit Help)
```

Displaying a description of the Search feature

Accessing Help from features and options

Another way you can use the Help feature is when you're actually using certain features. This is called context-sensitive help, which means that you can obtain information about a feature or option you're currently using. So, you don't have to exit to the normal editing screen or lose your place in a document in order to find the information you need.

Now let's try using context-sensitive help. First press 〔Enter〕 to return to the normal editing screen and then activate the Document Summary submenu of the Format menu by pressing 〔Shift〕+〔F8〕, 〔3〕, 〔5〕 or by activating the pull-down menus (〔Alt〕+〔=〕) or press the right mouse button) and selecting Summary from the File menu. The following should appear on your screen:

```
Document Summary

        Revision Date  06-02-91 07:12p

  1 - Creation Date  06-03-91 08:30p

  2 - Document Name
      Document Type

  3 - Author
      Typist

  4 - Subject

  5 - Account

  6 - Keywords

  7 - Abstract




Selection: 0              (Retrieve to capture; Del to remove summary)
```

The Document Summary submenu

To obtain information about this feature, press F3. The Document Summary help screen will appear.

```
┌─────────────────────────────────────────────────────────────────────────┐
│Document Summary                                                           │
│                                                                           │
│    Allows you to create or edit a document summary for a file.  You can   │
│    press Retrieve (Shift-F10) to have WordPerfect update the Subject and  │
│    Abstract fields.  To save the summary, press Save (F10).  To print the │
│    summary, press Print (Shift-F7).  You can also print the summary(ies)  │
│    from List Files.  The Document Management (Summary) feature (Setup, 3, 4)│
│    contains several options that affect the Document Summary feature.     │
│                                                                           │
│    Revision Date:  This is the date on which the file was last saved.     │
│                                                                           │
│    1 - Creation Date                                                      │
│                                                                           │
│    2 - Document Name/Document Type                                        │
│                                                                           │
│    3 - Author/Typist                                                      │
│                                                                           │
│    4 - Subject                                                            │
│                                                                           │
│    5 - Account                                                            │
│                                                                           │
│    6 - Keywords                                                           │
│                                                                           │
│    7 - Abstract                                                           │
│Selection: 0                                    (Press ENTER to exit Help) │
└─────────────────────────────────────────────────────────────────────────┘
```

The Document Summary help screen

Note:

Notice that the help screen and the actual submenu look very similar. Obviously this can be confusing when you're using context-sensitive help. To determine whether or not you're located in the help screen, look for the Press ENTER to exit Help message in the lower-right corner of your screen.

When you're finished with the help screen, press (Enter). This will return you to the Document Summary submenu. Then press Cancel ((F1)) until you reach the normal editing screen again.

You can also use context-sensitive help from the pull-down menus. Simply highlight the menu item for which you need information and press Help ((F3)). Let's try this now. Activate the menu bar by pressing (Alt)+(=) or by pressing the right mouse button and activate the File menu with the keyboard or mouse. Now highlight the Summary menu item by using the keyboard or the mouse.

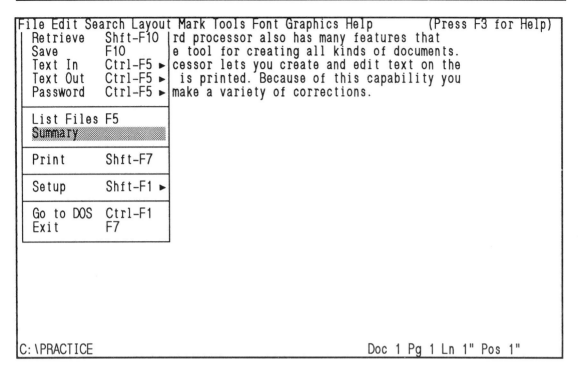

```
File Edit Search Layout Mark Tools Font Graphics Help        (Press F3 for Help)
 | Retrieve   Shft-F10 | rd processor also has many features that
 | Save       F10      | e tool for creating all kinds of documents.
 | Text In     Ctrl-F5 ► | cessor lets you create and edit text on the
 | Text Out    Ctrl-F5 ► |  is printed. Because of this capability you
 | Password    Ctrl-F5 ► | make a variety of corrections.
 |
 | List Files F5
 | Summary
 |
 | Print      Shft-F7
 |
 | Setup      Shft-F1 ►
 |
 | Go to DOS  Ctrl-F1
 | Exit       F7



C: \PRACTICE                                 Doc 1 Pg 1 Ln 1" Pos 1"
```

Summary highlighted in the File menu

When you press F3 the Document Summary help screen appears. Now press Enter; you will be returned to the File menu and the Summary item will still be highlighted.

Accessing the WordPerfect template

As we mentioned earlier in this book, you can display the WordPerfect template by pressing the F3 key twice. The template indicates to which feature each function key and key combination corresponds. If you're already located in either the list of features or a help screen for a specific feature, you can still access the template by pressing the F3 key once. To access the template from the pull-down menus, select Template from the Help menu.

The following tables list the key combinations, menu options and commands described in this chapter.

Key combination	Action
Alt + =	Activate pull-down menu
F1	Cancel
Shift + F1	Setup
F2	Search forward
Shift + F2	Search backward
F3	Help
F3, F3	Template
F5	List files (directory)
F7	Exit
Shift + F7	Print
Shift + F8	Format
Shift + F8, 3, 5	Document summary
F10	Save
Shift + F10	Retrieve

Menu selection	Action
Right mouse button	Activate pull-down menu
Right mouse button	Cancel
File/Setup	Setup
Search/Forward	Search forward
Search/Backward	Search backward
Help/Help	Help
Help/Template	Template
File/List Files	List files (directory)
File/Exit	Exit
File/Print	Print
Layout	Format
File/Summary	Document summary
File/Save	Save
File/Retrieve	Retrieve

4. Creating Your First Documents

Now that you're familiar with the WordPerfect environment and know how to access the basic commands, you should feel more comfortable working with the program. If you feel you still need more practice, review the previous chapters until you're ready to move on.

In this chapter, you'll learn how to create, format and edit documents. Instead of trying to explain each WordPerfect feature individually, we'll show you how to use some of the most common features through step-by-step examples in actual documents. This will allow you to become familiar with how the WordPerfect features operate. So, once you've completed the exercises in this book, you'll be able to create your own documents immediately. Also, you'll have a basis on which you can build your knowledge of WordPerfect.

Before we begin creating our document, we need to discuss some items that affect document formatting.

Default settings WordPerfect's normal editing screen is a *clean* screen. So, while you're working on your document, the way the text is displayed on the screen will basically be the way it will appear when printed. Since WordPerfect is designed for speed, this clean screen method enables the program to work quickly. The clean screen also enables you to create documents without being distracted by various menus and features.

When you create a new document, some basic formatting settings, such as margins, and configurations, such as screen display, are already established.

These are default settings and are used automatically by WordPerfect for all documents. You cannot see these settings on the screen or by using the Reveal Codes (Alt+F3) feature.

However, it's possible to change these settings by activating the appropriate feature and changing the setting. We'll show you how to do this in the next section.

Codes

While performing the examples in this chapter, many of the changes and settings you'll make will produce codes. Although these codes don't appear in the normal editing screen, WordPerfect uses them to determine how your text will appear when printed.

We'll discuss codes in more detail later in this chapter.

In order to use the examples in this chapter, you must type in the following text, exactly as it is shown. Don't worry if you see any mistakes—we'll correct them later in the chapter. Press (Enter) twice at the end of each paragraph:

```
To Our Shareholders

Current market conditions indicate that Trendy Togs, Inc. will continue
to build upon the gains displayed in this 1991 second
quarter report.

Profit climed 20% over first quarter. Sales are up 30%.
Stockholders' equity jumped by $400,000. The best news is the
company's ratio of current assests to current liabilities. It is now
3.0, a full 1.0 higher than this time last year.

The raw maerial remains stable, thanks to a strong domestic
supply. We have been told to expect price reductions in materials
over the next two quarters. THis will enable us to stabilize prices
for our customers and realize a larger profit.

The company recently purchased Baby Bottles, a local designer
diaper manufacturer. Baby Bottles has been relatively stagnant over
the last five years, but we fully intend to increase volume through
Trendy Togs' strong sales and distribution network within the next
year. This support, combined with Trendy Togs' new line of designer
baby clothes, should increase the profitability of Baby Bottles
tremendously.

K.J. Farnsworth
President
```

When you've entered the sample document, save it using the Save feature. Press Save ((F10)) or select Save from the File menu and enter the filename QUARTER. Press (Enter) to save the file under this name.

4.1 Document Formatting

In this section we'll make some formatting settings for our example document that will affect the entire document. We'll be using the Format feature to make these formatting settings.

Format feature

WordPerfect's Format feature enables you to make various kinds of formatting settings for your documents. The main format menu contains four submenus: Line, Page, Document and Other. Each of these menus contain various options for formatting your document.

Let's try using the Format feature now. To activate the main Format menu, either press [Shift]+[F 8] or activate the pull-down menus ([Alt]+[=]), select Line, Page, Document or Other from the Layout menu with the keyboard or mouse and press Cancel ([F1]). The following should appear:

```
Format

    1 - Line
              Hyphenation                Line Spacing
              Justification              Margins Left/Right
              Line Height                Tab Set
              Line Numbering             Widow/Orphan Protection

    2 - Page
              Center Page (top to bottom)   Page Numbering
              Force Odd/Even Page            Paper Size/Type
              Headers and Footers           Suppress
              Margins Top/Bottom

    3 - Document
              Display Pitch              Redline Method
              Initial Codes/Font         Summary

    4 - Other
              Advance                    Overstrike
              Conditional End of Page    Printer Functions
              Decimal Characters         Underline Spaces/Tabs
              Language                   Border Options

Selection: 0
```

Main Format menu

As you can see, each submenu offers a variety of options, which affect different aspects of your document. The options in the Line submenu affect the appearance of the lines, while the options in the Page submenu affect the way text appears in relation to the page. The Document submenu contains options that apply to the entire document and the Other submenu offers more advanced formatting features.

Now let's try activating one of these options. Select the Line submenu by pressing the ① or ⓛ keys or by positioning the mouse pointer on the option and clicking the left mouse button.

Note:　　To activate this option from the pull-down menus, select Line from the Layout menu with the keyboard or mouse.

To activate the Line Spacing option, press ⑥ or ⓢ or click the mouse button.

Notice that, depending on which key you pressed, a "6" or an "S" appears after `Selection:` in the status line. Also, the cursor is located on the "1" setting of the Line Spacing option.

```
Format: Line

    1 - Hyphenation                    No

    2 - Hyphenation Zone - Left        10%
                          Right        4%

    3 - Justification                  Full

    4 - Line Height                    Auto

    5 - Line Numbering                 No

    6 - Line Spacing                   1

    7 - Margins - Left                 1"
                 Right                 1"

    8 - Tab Set                        Rel; -1", every 0.5"

    9 - Widow/Orphan Protection        No



Selection: 6
```

Format Line submenu

This option sets the number of lines that are inserted each time the ⌜Enter⌟ key is pressed. So, if we wanted to use double-spaced lines, we would enter a "2" here.

For our document, let's use the default option, which is "1".

Press Exit (⌜F7⌟) or Cancel (⌜F1⌟) to leave the Line Spacing option. The cursor will return to the status line and a "0" will appear after Selection:.

Now let's activate the Hyphenation option by pressing ⌜1⌟ or ⌜Y⌟ or by positioning the mouse pointer on the option and clicking the left mouse button.

This option hyphenates words at the right margin. Using this option can improve the way text appears when it is printed. If the Hyphenation option is set to "No", WordPerfect moves (wraps) words, which extend beyond the right margin, to the next line.

```
Format: Line

   1 - Hyphenation                      No (Yes)

   2 - Hyphenation Zone - Left          10%
                          Right         4%

   3 - Justification                    Full

   4 - Line Height                      Auto

   5 - Line Numbering                   No

   6 - Line Spacing                     1

   7 - Margins - Left                   1"
                 Right                  1"

   8 - Tab Set                          Rel; -1", every 0.5"

   9 - Widow/Orphan Protection          No



Selection: 1
```

Hyphenation option activated

Again, notice that a "1" or "Y", depending on which key you pressed, appears in the Selection: line at the bottom of the screen and the cursor is located in the Hyphenation option.

Unlike the Line Spacing option, this setting is made by selecting "Yes" or "No".

Let's leave this option set to its default setting, which is "No", and return to the normal editing screen by pressing Exit ((F7)) or Cancel ((F1)).

Now that you know how the Format menu works, let's make some changes to our example document, QUARTER.

Setting margins

First let's determine the settings for the left and right margins of our document. WordPerfect measures margins from the left and right edges of a page. If you don't set the Margins Left/Right option, the default setting, which is "1" ", will be used for each side.

The Margins Left/Right option will affect a document from the current cursor position on. So the text that is located before the point where this option is set will not be affected.

We'll set our margins to "2"". Before activating the Format menu, be sure that the cursor is located at the beginning of the document. If the cursor is located at the end of the document, press the (Home) key twice and then press the (↑) key to move it to the beginning.

Note:

Moving the cursor to the beginning of the document is a very important step when establishing formatting settings that should affect your entire document.

Now activate the Format feature by pressing (Shift)+(F8). Then select the Line submenu by pressing (1) or (L) or by clicking on the option with a mouse.

Note:

You can activate the Format Line submenu directly by selecting Line from the Layout menu.

Next select the Margins Left/Right option by pressing (7) or (M) or by clicking with the mouse. Enter "2"" and press the (Enter) key. Then enter the same setting for the right margin.

```
Format: Line

    1 - Hyphenation                    No

    2 - Hyphenation Zone - Left        10%
                          Right        4%

    3 - Justification                  Full

    4 - Line Height                    Auto

    5 - Line Numbering                 No

    6 - Line Spacing                   1

    7 - Margins - Left                 2"
                  Right                2"

    8 - Tab Set                        Rel; -1", every 0.5"

    9 - Widow/Orphan Protection        No


Selection: 7
```

Setting the Margins Left/Right option

When you're finished, press (Enter) until the normal editing screen appears again. Notice that your text will be adjusted on the screen. The margins will be moved in from the left and right. If your screen does not look like the following illustration, press the ⊡ key a few times. If this does not reformat the text, your video drivers may be slightly different. This is nothing to worry about.

```
To Our Shareholders

Current market conditions indicate that Trendy
Togs, Inc. will continue to build upon the
gains displayed in this 1991 second quarter
report.

Profit climed 20% over first quarter. Sales
are up 30%. Stockholders' equity jumped by
$400,000. The best news is the company's ratio
of current assets to current liabilities. It
is now 3.0, a full 1.0 higher than this time
last year.

The raw maerial market remains stable, thanks
to a strong domestic supply. We have been told
to expect price reductions in materials over
the next two quarters. THis will enable us to
stabilize prices for our customers and realize
a larger profit.

The company recently purchased Baby Bottles, a
local designer diaper manufacturer. Baby
Bottles has been relatively stagnant over the
C:\QUARTER                                Doc 1 Pg 1 Ln 1" Pos 2"
```

Margins adjusted in example document

Centering the page

Now we'll make a formatting setting that will affect the entire page. This time we'll use the Page submenu to set the Center Page (top to bottom) option. This option centers the text of a document between the top and bottom margins so that there is an equal amount of space at the beginning and the end of a page. Obviously this setting is important for creating well-formatted letters.

Activate the Format feature by pressing (Shift)+(F8) and then select the Page submenu by pressing the (2) or (P) keys or by clicking with the mouse. The Format Page submenu should appear on your screen.

Note:

To activate the Format Page submenu directly, select Page from the Layout menu.

```
Format: Page

    1 - Center Page (top to bottom)    No

    2 - Force Odd/Even Page

    3 - Headers

    4 - Footers

    5 - Margins - Top                  1"
                  Bottom               1"

    6 - Page Numbering

    7 - Paper Size                     8.5" x 11"
                  Type                 Standard

    8 - Suppress (this page only)




Selection: 0
```

Format Page submenu

Now press the ①　or ⓒ　keys or click with the mouse to select the Center (top to bottom) option. Again notice that a "1" or "c" is displayed in the status line and the cursor appears in the option.

The default setting for this option is "No" or off. To switch on this option, press the Ⓨ　key for "Yes". To return to the main Format menu, press Cancel (F1) or Exit (F7).

Justifying text

The Justification option from the Line submenu of the Format feature aligns text to the margins of a document according to the following criteria:

Left:　　　　　The text is aligned to the left margin so the text at the right margin is uneven.

Center:　　　　The text is equally aligned between both margins.

Right:　　　　The text is aligned to the right margin so the text at the left margin is uneven.

Full: The text is aligned on both the left and right margins.

Now let's set the Justification option for our example document. First ensure that the cursor is located at the beginning of the document text. Then activate the Line submenu from the main Format menu by pressing ① or ⓛ or clicking with the mouse.

Note: To activate the Line submenu directly, select Line from the Layout menu.

Select the Justification option by pressing ③ or ⓙ or by clicking the mouse button. As you can see, this option is set to "Full", which is the default setting. Although this is the setting we want to use for our document, let's experiment with this option.

Notice that a menu appears, in the status line at the bottom of the screen, listing the settings that can be used.

```
Format: Line

     1 - Hyphenation                    No

     2 - Hyphenation Zone - Left        10%
                            Right       4%

     3 - Justification                  Full

     4 - Line Height                    Auto

     5 - Line Numbering                 No

     6 - Line Spacing                   1

     7 - Margins - Left                 1"
                   Right                1"

     8 - Tab Set                        Rel; -1", every 0.5"

     9 - Widow/Orphan Protection        No


Justification: 1 Left; 2 Center; 3 Right; 4 Full: 0
```

Justification options

Now select the Right option by pressing the ③ key and then the Enter key. Notice that "Right" appears in the Justification option. Press Enter until you reach the normal editing screen again.

The cursor should now be located at the right margin of your document. Using the ⊡ key, move the cursor to the end of the document.

```
                    ratio of current assets to current
        liabilities. It is now 3.0, a full 1.0 higher
                         than this time last year.

The raw maerial market remains stable, thanks to a
         strong domestic supply. We have been told to
         expect price reductions in materials over the
            next two quarters. THis will enable us to
             stabilize prices for our customers and
                         realize a larger profit.

     The company recently purchased Baby Bottles,
         a local designer diaper manufacturer. Baby
   Bottles has been relatively stagnant over the
            last five years, but we fully intend to
     increase volume through Trendy Togs' strong
          sales and distribution network within the
next year. This support, combined with Trendy
        Togs' new line of designer baby clothes,
       should increase the profitability of Baby
                         Bottles tremendously.

                              K.J. Farnsworth
                                   President
C:\QUARTER                  Doc 1 Pg 1 Ln 6.5" Pos 6.5"
```

Justification option set to Right

As you can see, the text is aligned to the right margin now and the text at the left margin is uneven. Obviously, this setting isn't suitable for our example document. So let's change the Justification setting back to "Full". However, before doing this, you must move the cursor back to the beginning of the document. To do this, use the ⬆ key. This is important because when this option is set it affects the text from the current cursor position on. So, the cursor must be located at the very beginning of the document in order to affect the entire document.

Now press (Shift)+(F8) to activate the Format feature and press (1) or (L) or click on the option with the mouse to activate the Line submenu or select Line from the Layout menu using the keyboard or mouse. Then activate the Justification option by pressing (3) or (J) or clicking with the mouse. To select the Full setting, press (4) and then press (Enter) until you reach the normal editing screen. Press the (↓) key until the cursor reaches the end of the document.

Of all the settings that can be selected for the Justification option, only Full isn't represented on the normal editing screen. So when this setting is selected, the way your document's text is aligned on the screen is not the way it will appear when the document is printed.

Revealing and deleting codes

As we mentioned earlier, invisible codes are inserted in documents for many of the formatting settings you make. In the previous section, we used the Format feature and its options to set the left and right margins, center the page and justify the text. All of these settings inserted a code into our sample document.

Let's display the codes for our sample document now. To do this, activate the Reveal Codes feature by pressing (Alt)+(F3) or by activating the pull-down menu and selecting Reveal Codes from the Edit menu either with the keyboard or the mouse. You should see the following or similar information on your screen:

```
┌─────────────────────────────────────────────────────────────────┐
│       To Our Shareholders                                         │
│                                                                   │
│       Current market conditions indicate that Trendy              │
│       Togs, Inc. will continue to build upon the                  │
│       gains displayed in this 1991 second quarter                 │
│       report.                                                     │
│                                                                   │
│       Profit climed 20% over first quarter. Sales                 │
│       are up 30%. Stockholders' equity jumped by                  │
│       $400,000. The best news is the company's ratio              │
│       of current assets to current liabilities. It               │
│ C:\QUARTER                                      Doc 1 Pg 1 Ln 1" Pos 2" │
│ ^     ^    ^    ^    ^    ^     ^    ^        ^   ^      ^     ^    │
│      {                                       }                    │
│ [Just:Right][Just:Full][L/R Mar:2",2"][Center Pg]To Our Shareholders[HRt] │
│ [HRt]                                                             │
│ Current market conditions indicate that Trendy[SRt]              │
│ Togs, Inc. will continue to build upon the[SRt]                  │
│ gains displayed in this 1991 second quarter[SRt]                 │
│ report.[HRt]                                                      │
│ [HRt]                                                             │
│ Profit climed 20% over first quarter. Sales[SRt]                │
│ are up 30%. Stockholders' equity jumped by[SRt]                  │
│ $400,000. The best news is the company's ratio[SRt]             │
│                                                                   │
│ Press Reveal Codes to restore screen                             │
└─────────────────────────────────────────────────────────────────┘
```

Reveal Codes screen

As you can see, a ruler containing tab markers (triangles) divides your screen into two sections. The top of the screen displays the normal editing screen and the bottom half shows the text of the normal editing screen and the codes that have been inserted into the document. Usually the margins are represented on the ruler by brackets [], but in our document they are represented by braces { }. This happened because our margin settings are located on tab settings.

Also notice that the cursor is located in the same position in both parts of the screen. In the normal editing screen the cursor is a blinking dash but in the Reveal Codes screen the cursor is a rectangle that highlights the character on which it is currently located. When you move the cursor in the normal editing screen it will also move to the same position in the Reveal Codes screen.

If you look at the codes that are displayed, you'll see that one was inserted for each of the formatting settings we made in the previous section—Justification, Margins and Center Page.

Deleting codes   However, although we changed the Justification option from the Right setting back to Full, the Right Justification code was inserted as a code and will remain in our document unless it is deleted. This demonstrates that every setting made in a document is inserted as a code even if you change the setting later. So it is important that you delete unnecessary codes from your documents because they may cause problems.

Now let's delete the Right Justification code from our document. To do this, highlight the [Just:Right] code by moving the cursor with the arrow keys.

```
To Our Shareholders

Current market conditions indicate that Trendy
Togs, Inc. will continue to build upon the
gains displayed in this 1991 second quarter
report.

Profit climed 20% over first quarter. Sales
are up 30%. Stockholders' equity jumped by
$400,000. The best news is the company's ratio
of current assets to current liabilities. It
C:\QUARTER                                Doc 1 Pg 1 Ln 1" Pos 1"
{     ^    ^    ^    ^    ^    ^    ^    ^    ^    }   ^    ^
[Just:Right][Just:Full][L/R Mar:2",2"][Center Pg]To Our Shareholders[HRt]
[HRt]
Current market conditions indicate that Trendy[SRt]
Togs, Inc. will continue to build upon the[SRt]
gains displayed in this 1991 second quarter[SRt]
report.[HRt]
[HRt]
Profit climed 20% over first quarter. Sales[SRt]
are up 30%. Stockholders' equity jumped by[SRt]
$400,000. The best news is the company's ratio[SRt]

Press Reveal Codes to restore screen
```

The Right Justification code selected

Then press the Del key to remove the code. To return to the normal editing screen, press Reveal Codes (Alt+F3) again.

The following is a summary of the commands discussed in this section.

Action	Key combination
Cancel	F1
Center Page (top/bottom)	Shift+F8, 2, 1
	Shift+F8, P, C
Exit	F7
Format Line	Shift+F8, 1
	Shift+F8, L
Format Page	Shift+F8, 2
	Shift+F8, P
Hyphenation	Shift+F8, 1, 1
	Shift+F8, L, Y
Justification	Shift+F8, 1, 3
	Shift+F8, L, J
Line Spacing	Shift+F8, 1, 6
	Shift+F8, L, S
Margins Left/Right	Shift+F8, 1, 7
	Shift+F8, L, M
Page	Shift+F8, 2
	Shift+F8, P
Pull-down menus	Alt+=
Reveal Codes	Alt+F3
Save	F10

Action	Menu selection
Cancel	Right mouse button
Center Page (top/bottom)	Layout/Page/Center Page
Exit	File/Exit
Format Line	Layout/Line
Format Page	Layout/Page
Hyphenation	Layout/Line/Hyphenation
Justification	Layout/Line/Justification
Line Spacing	Layout/Line/Line Spacing
Margins Left/Right	Layout/Line/Margins
Pull-down menus	Right mouse button
Reveal Codes	Edit/Reveal Codes
Save	File/Save

4.2 Text Formatting

In this section we'll make some formatting changes in our sample document that will affect specific characters or sections of text. These formatting changes differ from settings you made in the previous section because, instead of the entire document, only certain characters will be affected by the settings.

These types of changes, such as underlining and bold, help draw attention to certain aspects of your documents. This enables you to create documents that are interesting and effective. Having these features available is one of the advantages of using a word processor such as WordPerfect.

Block feature

The Block feature allows you to select a character, several characters or an entire paragraph so that it can be used with another WordPerfect feature. By doing this, you can create a document, without selecting any formatting settings, and then go back and format the existing text later. The Block feature can be used with many WordPerfect features, such as Bold, Delete, Justification and Sort. For a complete list of features, consult your WordPerfect manual.

Note:

Although we are demonstrating how to set certain formatting features after a document has been created, remember that it's also possible to make these settings while you're creating your document. Basically you would use the same methods described here except that you wouldn't need the Block feature to select the text. Instead, you would select the appropriate formatting setting, type your text and then switch off any codes that may have been inserted. To switch off a code, either select the appropriate setting again or move the cursor past the off code in the Reveal Codes screen. (For more information consult your WordPerfect manual.)

In this section, we'll use Block in several ways so that you can learn how to use this important WordPerfect feature. As you will see, it is easy to use and can be used in a variety of ways.

Now let's try using Block. The first change we'll make to our document is to set the first line, "To Our Shareholders", to all uppercase characters. This will help draw attention to this line.

Note: Although it's possible to create uppercase characters when entering text by pressing the Shift key or by activating the Caps Lock key, you can use the Block feature to do the same thing with existing text.

First move the cursor, with the arrow keys, to the beginning of the first line in our document. Turn on the Block feature by pressing Alt + F4 or by selecting Block from the Edit menu using the keyboard or the mouse.

The Block on message will begin to flash in the status line at the lower-left corner of your screen.

```
To Our Shareholders

Current market conditions indicate that Trendy
Togs, Inc. will continue to build upon the
gains displayed in this 1991 second quarter
report.

Profit climed 20% over first quarter. Sales
are up 30%. Stockholders' equity jumped by
$400,000. The best news is the company's ratio
of current assets to current liabilities. It
is now 3.0, a full 1.0 higher than this time
last year.

The raw maerial market remains stable, thanks
to a strong domestic supply. We have been told
to expect price reductions in materials over
the next two quarters. THis will enable us to
stabilize prices for our customers and realize
a larger profit.

The company recently purchased Baby Bottles, a
local designer diaper manufacturer. Baby
Bottles has been relatively stagnant over the
Block on                                   Doc 1 Pg 1 Ln 1" Pos 2"
```

Activating the Block feature

To select the text that we want to format, press the → key until you reach the end of the line. Or to select the text with a mouse, position the pointer on one end of the line to be blocked and press the left mouse button. Then, while holding down the mouse button, move the mouse pointer to the opposite end of the line and release the mouse button.

To Our Shareholders

Current market conditions indicate that Trendy
Togs, Inc. will continue to build upon the
gains displayed in this 1991 second quarter
report.

Profit climed 20% over first quarter. Sales
are up 30%. Stockholders' equity jumped by
$400,000. The best news is the company's ratio
of current assets to current liabilities. It
is now 3.0, a full 1.0 higher than this time
last year.

The raw maerial market remains stable, thanks
to a strong domestic supply. We have been told
to expect price reductions in materials over
the next two quarters. THis will enable us to
stabilize prices for our customers and realize
a larger profit.

The company recently purchased Baby Bottles, a
local designer diaper manufacturer. Baby
Bottles has been relatively stagnant over the

Block on   Doc 1 Pg 1 Ln 1" Pos 3.9"

Selecting text to be blocked

As you move the cursor or mouse, the text is highlighted, which means it is displayed in reverse video. This highlighted section of text is called a *block*. Now let's select the appropriate feature.

In order to change all the characters to uppercase, activate the Switch feature by pressing Shift + F3 or select Convert Case from the Edit menu using the keyboard or the mouse. In the status line, a menu, containing the options Uppercase and Lowercase, appears. Select the Uppercase option by pressing the 1 or U keys.

Notice that the Block feature is automatically turned off when a feature is selected.

If you want to cancel the Block feature without selecting any features, simply press Block (Alt + F4) again or press Cancel (F1).

The first line of our sample document should now look as follows:

```
TO OUR SHAREHOLDERS

Current market conditions indicate that Trendy
Togs, Inc. will continue to build upon the
gains displayed in this 1991 second quarter
report.

Profit climed 20% over first quarter. Sales
are up 30%. Stockholders' equity jumped by
$400,000. The best news is the company's ratio
of current assets to current liabilities. It
is now 3.0, a full 1.0 higher than this time
last year.

The raw maerial market remains stable, thanks
to a strong domestic supply. We have been told
to expect price reductions in materials over
the next two quarters. THis will enable us to
stabilize prices for our customers and realize
a larger profit.

The company recently purchased Baby Bottles, a
local designer diaper manufacturer. Baby
Bottles has been relatively stagnant over the
```
C:\QUARTER   Doc 1 Pg 1 Ln 1" Pos 3.9"

All characters changed to uppercase

Now that you've used the Block feature, we'll make some additional changes to our document using various features.

Changing the font size

In addition to making all the characters in the first line uppercase, we also want to change the actual size of the characters. This will make them stand out from the other characters in the document and will emphasize the first line.

To do this, first move the cursor to the beginning of the line and activate the Block feature by pressing [Alt]+[F4] or by selecting Block from the Edit menu. Then select the entire line by pressing the [→] key or by using the mouse, as previously explained.

Note:

In this example we'll explain the keyboard and pull-down menu methods separately.

Next activate the Font feature by pressing [Ctrl]+[F8]. The Font menu will appear in the status line at the bottom of your screen.

```
┌──────────────────────────────────────────────────────────────┐
│          ▓TO OUR SHAREHOLDERS▓                                 │
│                                                                │
│      Current market conditions indicate that Trendy            │
│      Togs, Inc. will continue to build upon the                │
│      gains displayed in this 1991 second quarter               │
│      report.                                                   │
│                                                                │
│      Profit climed 20% over first quarter. Sales               │
│      are up 30%. Stockholders' equity jumped by                │
│      $400,000. The best news is the company's ratio            │
│      of current assets to current liabilities. It              │
│      is now 3.0, a full 1.0 higher than this time              │
│      last year.                                                │
│                                                                │
│      The raw maerial market remains stable, thanks             │
│      to a strong domestic supply. We have been told            │
│      to expect price reductions in materials over              │
│      the next two quarters. THis will enable us to             │
│      stabilize prices for our customers and realize            │
│      a larger profit.                                          │
│                                                                │
│      The company recently purchased Baby Bottles, a            │
│      local designer diaper manufacturer. Baby                  │
│      Bottles has been relatively stagnant over the             │
│Attribute: 1 Size; 2 Appearance: 0                              │
└──────────────────────────────────────────────────────────────┘
```

Activating the Font feature

This menu displays the attributes that can be used to change the way text appears when it is printed. The Size attributes determine the size of the characters and the Appearance attributes determine how characters look on the page.

Let's select the Size option by pressing ⒈ or Ⓢ. Another menu, listing the Size options, appears. Select the Very Large option by pressing ⒍ or Ⓥ.

To change the font size using the pull-down menus, simply select Very Large from the Font menu.

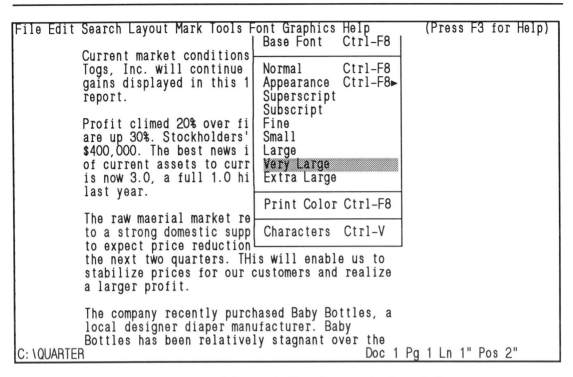

File Edit Search Layout Mark Tools Font Graphics Help   (Press F3 for Help)

	Base Font Ctrl-F8	

Current market conditions
Togs, Inc. will continue   Normal   Ctrl-F8
gains displayed in this 1   Appearance   Ctrl-F8▶
report.   Superscript
                             Subscript
Profit climed 20% over fi   Fine
are up 30%. Stockholders'   Small
$400,000. The best news i   Large
of current assets to curr   Very Large
is now 3.0, a full 1.0 hi   Extra Large
last year.
                             Print Color Ctrl-F8
The raw maerial market re
to a strong domestic supp   Characters Ctrl-V
to expect price reduction
the next two quarters. THis will enable us to
stabilize prices for our customers and realize
a larger profit.

The company recently purchased Baby Bottles, a
local designer diaper manufacturer. Baby
Bottles has been relatively stagnant over the

C:\QUARTER   Doc 1 Pg 1 Ln 1" Pos 2"

Selecting the Very Large option from the Font menu

As you can see, no change appears on the screen but the text is highlighted and a code is inserted before and after the block. Let's activate Reveal Codes so that we can see these codes inserted in our document. Press Reveal Codes (Alt + F3) or select Reveal Codes from the Edit menu with the keyboard or the mouse. Your screen should look similar to the following:

```
     TO OUR SHAREHOLDERS
          Current market conditions indicate that Trendy
          Togs, Inc. will continue to build upon the
          gains displayed in this 1991 second quarter
          report.

          Profit climed 20% over first quarter. Sales
          are up 30%. Stockholders' equity jumped by
          $400,000. The best news is the company's ratio
          of current assets to current liabilities. It
C:\QUARTER                                        Doc 1 Pg 1 Ln 1" Pos 3.9"
-     -   {                                         }
[Just:Full][L/R Mar:2",2"][Center Pg][VRY LARGE]TO OUR SHAREHOLDERS[vry large][H
Rt]
[HRt]
Current market conditions indicate that Trendy[SRt]
Togs, Inc. will continue to build upon the[SRt]
gains displayed in this 1991 second quarter[SRt]
report.[HRt]
[HRt]
Profit climed 20% over first quarter. Sales[SRt]
are up 30%. Stockholders' equity jumped by[SRt]

Press Reveal Codes to restore screen
```

Activating the Reveal Codes screen

Notice that the [VRY LARGE] code is displayed twice—before and after the line that was blocked. As you may remember, earlier in this book we mentioned paired codes, which work together to signify "on" and "off". When a paired code is displayed in all uppercase letters, as in the example above, the code is switched on, and when the code is displayed in all lowercase letters, the code is switched off.

Now let's return to the normal editing screen by activating Reveal Codes again.

Underlining text

Let's continue to format the first line of our document since there are many more features we can use to make this line stand out from the rest of the text. For example, let's underline the characters.

First move the cursor to the beginning of the line. Then activate the Block feature by pressing (Alt)+(F4) or by selecting Block from the Edit menu. Select the entire line either with the arrow keys or with the mouse. Now activate the Underline feature by pressing (F8).

To activate Underline from the the pull-down menus, with the keyboard or mouse select Appearance from the Font menu and then select Underline.

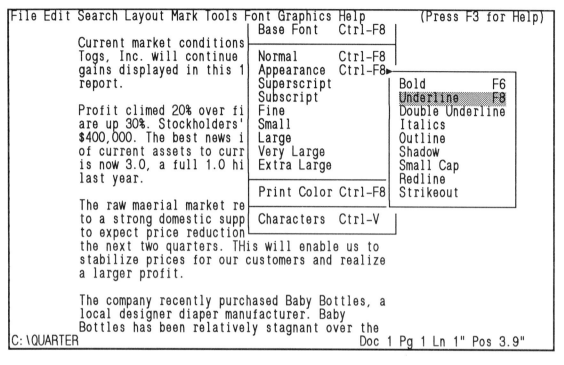

```
File Edit Search Layout Mark Tools Font Graphics Help        (Press F3 for Help)
                                      Base Font   Ctrl-F8 |
            Current market conditions |                   |
            Togs, Inc. will continue  | Normal      Ctrl-F8 |
            gains displayed in this 1 | Appearance  Ctrl-F8▶
            report.                   | Superscript        | Bold          F6
                                      | Subscript          | Underline     F8
            Profit climed 20% over fi | Fine               | Double Underline
            are up 30%. Stockholders' | Small              | Italics
            $400,000. The best news i | Large              | Outline
            of current assets to curr | Very Large         | Shadow
            is now 3.0, a full 1.0 hi | Extra Large        | Small Cap
            last year.                |_____| Redline
                                      | Print Color Ctrl-F8| Strikeout
            The raw maerial market re |                    |
            to a strong domestic supp | Characters   Ctrl-V |
            to expect price reduction |_____|
            the next two quarters. THis will enable us to
            stabilize prices for our customers and realize
            a larger profit.

            The company recently purchased Baby Bottles, a
            local designer diaper manufacturer. Baby
            Bottles has been relatively stagnant over the
C:\QUARTER                                    Doc 1 Pg 1 Ln 1" Pos 3.9"
```

Selecting the Underline feature

As you can see, no changes were made to the text on the normal editing screen.

However, if you look at the status line, you'll see that the position number of the cursor is highlighted.

```
┌─────────────────────────────────────────────────────────────────┐
│      TO OUR SHAREHOLDERS                                          │
│                                                                   │
│      Current market conditions indicate that Trendy              │
│      Togs, Inc. will continue to build upon the                  │
│      gains displayed in this 1991 second quarter                 │
│      report.                                                      │
│                                                                   │
│      Profit climed 20% over first quarter. Sales                 │
│      are up 30%. Stockholders' equity jumped by                  │
│      $400,000. The best news is the company's ratio              │
│      of current assets to current liabilities. It                │
│      is now 3.0, a full 1.0 higher than this time                │
│      last year.                                                   │
│                                                                   │
│      The raw maerial market remains stable, thanks               │
│      to a strong domestic supply. We have been told              │
│      to expect price reductions in materials over                │
│      the next two quarters. THis will enable us to               │
│      stabilize prices for our customers and realize              │
│      a larger profit.                                             │
│                                                                   │
│      The company recently purchased Baby Bottles, a              │
│      local designer diaper manufacturer. Baby                    │
│      Bottles has been relatively stagnant over the               │
│ C:\QUARTER                              Doc 1 Pg 1 Ln 1" Pos 3.9" │
└─────────────────────────────────────────────────────────────────┘
```

Underline feature activated

This indicates that the feature has been activated. Now let's activate Reveal Codes to see that the Underline code was inserted in the document. Press Alt + F3 or select Reveal Codes from the Edit menu. The following should appear on your screen:

```
┌──────────────────────────────────────────────────────────────────────┐
│        TO OUR SHAREHOLDERS                                             │
│        Current market conditions indicate that Trendy                  │
│        Togs, Inc. will continue to build upon the                      │
│        gains displayed in this 1991 second quarter                     │
│        report.                                                         │
│                                                                        │
│        Profit climed 20% over first quarter. Sales                     │
│        are up 30%. Stockholders' equity jumped by                      │
│        $400,000. The best news is the company's ratio                  │
│        of current assets to current liabilities. It                    │
│C:\QUARTER                                    Doc 1 Pg 1 Ln 1" Pos 3.9"  │
│─  ─  {   ^   ^   ^   ^   ^   ^   ^   ^  }                               │
│[Just:Full][L/R Mar:2",2"][Center Pg][VRY LARGE][UND]TO OUR SHAREHOLDERS[und][vr│
│y large][HRt]                                                           │
│[HRt]                                                                   │
│Current market conditions indicate that Trendy[SRt]                     │
│Togs, Inc. will continue to build upon the[SRt]                         │
│gains displayed in this 1991 second quarter[SRt]                        │
│report.[HRt]                                                            │
│[HRt]                                                                   │
│Profit climed 20% over first quarter. Sales[SRt]                        │
│are up 30%. Stockholders' equity jumped by[SRt]                         │
│                                                                        │
│Press Reveal Codes to restore screen                                    │
└──────────────────────────────────────────────────────────────────────┘
```

Displaying the Underline code

Notice that the [UND] code, which switches on the Underline feature, appears before the line and the [und] code, which switches off this feature, appears after the line.

To return to the normal editing screen, activate the Reveal Codes feature again by pressing Alt + F3 or by selecting Reveal Codes from the Edit menu with the keyboard or mouse.

Bold text

Now let's change the characters in the first line to bold text. When you use the Bold feature, the characters that are affected will be printed in darker print than the other characters in the document.

First move the cursor to the beginning of the line and then activate the Block feature by pressing Alt + F4 or selecting Block from the Edit menu with the keyboard or the mouse. Then select the line by using the arrow keys or the mouse.

Now activate the Bold feature by pressing F6.

To use the pull-down menus to select this feature, select Appearance from the Font menu and select Bold.

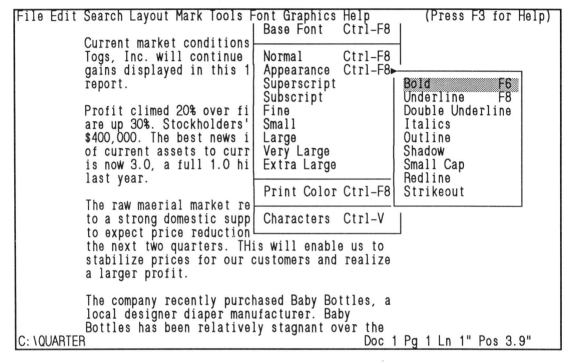

Activating the Bold feature

Notice that the selected text appears in reverse video in a highlighted section of the screen. Also, the position number of the cursor is highlighted in the status line, which indicates that the feature is activated.

```
┌─────────────────────────────────────────────────────────────┐
│  TO OUR SHAREHOLDERS                                          │
│                                                               │
│  Current market conditions indicate that Trendy              │
│  Togs, Inc. will continue to build upon the                  │
│  gains displayed in this 1991 second quarter                 │
│  report.                                                      │
│                                                               │
│  Profit climed 20% over first quarter. Sales                 │
│  are up 30%. Stockholders' equity jumped by                  │
│  $400,000. The best news is the company's ratio              │
│  of current assets to current liabilities. It                │
│  is now 3.0, a full 1.0 higher than this time                │
│  last year.                                                   │
│                                                               │
│  The raw maerial market remains stable, thanks               │
│  to a strong domestic supply. We have been told              │
│  to expect price reductions in materials over                │
│  the next two quarters. THis will enable us to               │
│  stabilize prices for our customers and realize              │
│  a larger profit.                                             │
│                                                               │
│  The company recently purchased Baby Bottles, a              │
│  local designer diaper manufacturer. Baby                    │
│  Bottles has been relatively stagnant over the               │
│ C:\QUARTER                        Doc 1 Pg 1 Ln 1" Pos 3.9"   │
└─────────────────────────────────────────────────────────────┘
```

Bold feature activated

To display the Bold code that was inserted in your document, activate Reveal Codes by pressing `Alt`+`F3` or by selecting Reveal Codes from the Edit menu. As you can see, the Bold code is inserted before and after the line. To return to the normal editing screen, activate Reveal Codes again.

Now let's try using the Bold feature on one character instead of the entire line.

Move the cursor to the "C" in the first line of the first paragraph of the document. Then activate the Block feature by pressing `Alt`+`F4` or by selecting Block from the Edit menu with the keyboard or mouse. Select the letter by pressing the `→` key once or clicking with the mouse.

Activate the Bold feature by pressing `F6` or by selecting Appearance from the Font menu and then selecting Bold.

```
┌──────────────────────────────────────────────────────────────────────────┐
│        TO OUR SHAREHOLDERS                                                 │
│                                                                            │
│        Current market conditions indicate that Trendy                      │
│        Togs, Inc. will continue to build upon the                          │
│        gains displayed in this 1991 second quarter                         │
│        report.                                                             │
│                                                                            │
│        Profit climed 20% over first quarter. Sales                         │
│        are up 30%. Stockholders' equity jumped by                          │
│        $400,000. The best news is the company's ratio                      │
│        of current assets to current liabilities. It                        │
│        is now 3.0, a full 1.0 higher than this time                        │
│        last year.                                                          │
│                                                                            │
│        The raw maerial market remains stable, thanks                       │
│        to a strong domestic supply. We have been told                      │
│        to expect price reductions in materials over                        │
│        the next two quarters. THis will enable us to                       │
│        stabilize prices for our customers and realize                      │
│        a larger profit.                                                    │
│                                                                            │
│        The company recently purchased Baby Bottles, a                      │
│        local designer diaper manufacturer. Baby                            │
│        Bottles has been relatively stagnant over the                       │
│ C:\QUARTER                                   Doc 1 Pg 1 Ln 1.33" Pos 2.1"   │
└──────────────────────────────────────────────────────────────────────────┘
```

Changing one character to bold text

Notice that the "C" is now enhanced on your screen. This indicates that the Bold feature is activated.

Indenting lines

The Indent feature enables you to indent paragraphs without changing the margin settings of your document. Indent does this by setting a temporary left margin at the next tab setting for an entire paragraph. Although pressing the `Tab` key also indents lines, the Indent feature allows you to indent entire paragraphs.

So you don't have to press `Tab` for each line that you want to indent.

Note:

We'll discuss tabs later in this chapter.

There are various ways you can indent text. You can select the Left option, which indents only the left margin of the paragraph, the Double option, which indents both margins of the paragraph, and the Hanging option, which indents all the lines except the first line of the paragraph.

Since the second paragraph of our document contains some very important information, let's emphasize this paragraph by making some formatting changes. One way to do this is to indent both margins of the paragraph.

First move the cursor to the first letter ("P") of the second paragraph. Then activate the Indent Left and Right feature by pressing [Shift]+[F4]. To use the pull-down menus, select Align from the Layout menu and then select Indent -><- using the keyboard or the mouse.

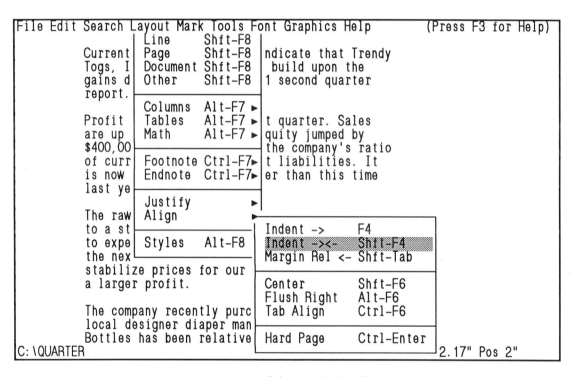

Selecting the Double Indent option

Once this feature is activated, the left and right margins of the paragraph are indented. Press the [↓] key to see the format change. Also, notice that the cursor position number in the status line has changed from 2" to 2.5".

```
┌──────────────────────────────────────────────────────────────┐
│          TO OUR SHAREHOLDERS                                   │
│                                                                │
│          Current market conditions indicate that Trendy        │
│          Togs, Inc. will continue to build upon the            │
│          gains displayed in this 1991 second quarter           │
│          report.                                               │
│                                                                │
│                    Profit climed 20% over first                │
│                    quarter. Sales are up 30%.                  │
│                    Stockholders' equity jumped by              │
│                    $400,000. The best news is the              │
│                    company's ratio of current assets to        │
│                    current liabilities. It is now 3.0,         │
│                    a full 1.0 higher than this time            │
│                    last year.                                  │
│                                                                │
│          The raw maerial market remains stable, thanks         │
│          to a strong domestic supply. We have been told        │
│          to expect price reductions in materials over          │
│          the next two quarters. THis will enable us to         │
│          stabilize prices for our customers and realize        │
│          a larger profit.                                      │
│                                                                │
│          The company recently purchased Baby Bottles, a        │
│ C:\QUARTER                              Doc 1 Pg 1 Ln 2.17" Pos 2.5" │
└──────────────────────────────────────────────────────────────┘
```

Paragraph indented with the Indent feature

Now activate Reveal Codes by pressing [Alt]+[F3] or selecting Reveal Codes from the Edit menu. As you can see, the Indent code was inserted before the second paragraph.

However, notice that the code appears only at the beginning of the paragraph and not at the end as we've previously seen. This occurred because this code is automatically switched off when it encounters a Hard Return code ([HRt]).

Let's discuss Hard Returns and Soft Returns briefly. If you look at the Reveal Codes screen, you'll see that there are Soft Returns, which are represented as [SRt], and Hard Returns, which are represented as [HRt]. While WordPerfect automatically inserts Soft Returns, Hard Returns are inserted by the user to signify the end of a paragraph, or to insert a blank line in a document.

Flush Right   For our next formatting change, we'll move to the end of our document. Let's align the president's name and title to the right margin. To do this, move the cursor to the "K" of the president's name. Activate the Block feature by pressing [Alt]+[F4] or by selecting Block from the Edit menu using the keyboard or the mouse.

Now select the name and title by pressing the [→] and [↓] key or by clicking with the mouse until both lines are displayed in reverse video. Then select the Flush Right feature by pressing [Alt]+[F6].

A prompt, asking you to confirm the Flush Right selection, will appear in the status line at the bottom of the screen. Press [Y] to confirm.

To use the pull-down menu to activate this feature, select Align from the Layout menu and then select Flush Right.

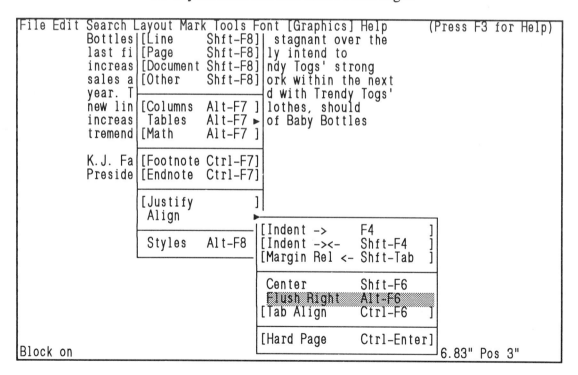

Selecting the Flush Right feature

Once the feature is activated, your screen should look similar to the following:

```
                    a full 1.0 higher than this time
                    last year.

                    The raw maerial market remains stable, thanks
                    to a strong domestic supply. We have been told
                    to expect price reductions in materials over
                    the next two quarters. THis will enable us to
                    stabilize prices for our customers and realize
                    a larger profit.

                    The company recently purchased Baby Bottles, a
                    local designer diaper manufacturer. Baby
                    Bottles has been relatively stagnant over the
                    last five years, but we fully intend to
                    increase volume through Trendy Togs' strong
                    sales and distribution network within the next
                    year. This support, combined with Trendy Togs'
                    new line of designer baby clothes, should
                    increase the profitability of Baby Bottles
                    tremendously.

                                         K.J. Farnsworth
                                         President

C:\QUARTER                              Doc 1 Pg 1 Ln 7.08" Pos 2"
```

Moving text to right margin

As you can see, the president's name and title have been moved to the right margin of the document.

Now let's activate Reveal Codes to see that the Flush Right code was inserted in the document. To do this, press Alt + F3 or select Reveal Codes from the Edit menu.

Notice that the [Just:Right] code is inserted before the president's name and the Justification Full code is placed after the title. This is similar to the Indent feature we used in the previous section. The Flush Right feature is also automatically switched off when a Hard return code is encountered. The Justification Full code is placed after the title because this matches the justification that was set for the entire document.

To return to the normal editing screen, activate Reveal Codes again by pressing Alt + F3 or selecting Reveal Codes from the Edit menu.

The text formatting for our document is now complete. To retain the changes you've made, save your document by activating the Save feature. Either press [F10] or select Save from the File menu with the keyboard or mouse. Then press [Enter] and [Y].

The following tables list the key combinations and menu options of commands discussed in this section.

Action	Key combination
Block	[Alt]+[F4]
Bold	[F6]
Flush Right	[Alt]+[F6]
Font	[Ctrl]+[F8]
Indent Left & Right	[Shift]+[F4]
Save	[F10]
Switch case	[Shift]+[F3]
Very large font size	[Ctrl]+[F8],[1],[6]
	[Ctrl]+[F8],[S],[V]

Action	Menu selection
Block	Edit/Block
Bold	Font/Appearance/Bold
Flush Right	Layout/Align/Flush Right
Font	Font/Appearance/Bold
Indent Left & Right	Layout/Align/Indent -><
Save	File/Save
Switch case	Edit/Convert Case
Very large font size	Font/Very Large

4.3 Editing Your Document

Once you've completed a document and made the necessary formatting settings, you should edit your document. This process involves making various changes to the document. For example, when you edit your document you can correct spelling errors and move text to different locations.

In this section, we'll show you how to use some of the WordPerfect features that can be used to edit your documents. By using these and other features, you'll be able to create quality documents.

Moving text

WordPerfect's Move feature enables you to move, copy and delete sections of text.

This is very useful if, after reading through a document, you realize that a certain word, sentence or paragraph would be more effective in a different location or should be removed from the document.

For example, in our sample document QUARTER, the fourth paragraph would be more effective if it was located where the third paragraph is currently located. Fortunately, this is very easy to do with WordPerfect.

First move the cursor to the line before the first line of the fourth paragraph. Then activate the Block feature by pressing Alt + F4 or by selecting Block from the Edit menu using the keyboard or mouse. The Block message will begin to flash in the lower-left corner of your screen. Now select the fourth paragraph by pressing the ↓ key or with the mouse until the entire paragraph is highlighted.

Note:

Although we're using the Block feature to select the text to be moved, the Move feature can also be used to select the text.

```
        a full 1.0 higher than this time
        last year.

    The raw maerial market remains stable, thanks
    to a strong domestic supply. We have been told
    to expect price reductions in materials over
    the next two quarters. THis will enable us to
    stabilize prices for our customers and realize
    a larger profit.

    The company recently purchased Baby Bottles, a
    local designer diaper manufacturer. Baby
    Bottles has been relatively stagnant over the
    last five years, but we fully intend to
    increase volume through Trendy Togs' strong
    sales and distribution network within the next
    year. This support, combined with Trendy Togs'
    new line of designer baby clothes, should
    increase the profitability of Baby Bottles
    tremendously.

                        K.J. Farnsworth
                        President
```

Block on   Doc 1 Pg 1 Ln 6.5" Pos 2"

Using Block to select a paragraph

Note: From this point on the function key method and pull-down menu
              method differ for this feature. So we'll explain them separately.

              Now activate the Move feature by pressing ⌈Ctrl⌉+⌈F4⌉. A menu
              appears in the status line at the bottom of the screen. The options in
              this menu indicate the type of block that will be moved. Select the
              Block option by pressing ⌈1⌉ or ⌈B⌉ . Another menu, containing the
              Move options, appears in the status line.

```
    a full 1.0 higher than this time
    last year.

The raw maerial market remains stable, thanks
to a strong domestic supply. We have been told
to expect price reductions in materials over
the next two quarters. THis will enable us to
stabilize prices for our customers and realize
a larger profit.

The company recently purchased Baby Bottles, a
local designer diaper manufacturer. Baby
Bottles has been relatively stagnant over the
last five years, but we fully intend to
increase volume through Trendy Togs' strong
sales and distribution network within the next
year. This support, combined with Trendy Togs'
new line of designer baby clothes, should
increase the profitability of Baby Bottles
tremendously.

                              K.J. Farnsworth
                              President
1 Move; 2 Copy; 3 Delete; 4 Append: 0
```

Move options

If the Move option is selected, the blocked text is removed from the screen.

If the Copy option is selected, the blocked text remains on the screen. Selecting either one of these options places the blocked text in a temporary buffer. The Delete option deletes the text from the screen and the Append option enables you to move the blocked text to an existing file that is saved on disk.

Since we want to move our paragraph to a different location, select the Move option by pressing ① or Ⓜ.

If you're using the pull-down menus, select Move (Cut) from the Edit menu with either the keyboard or mouse.

The paragraph disappears from the screen and a prompt message appears in the status line.

```
Current market conditions indicate that Trendy
Togs, Inc. will continue to build upon the
gains displayed in this 1991 second quarter
report.

        Profit climed 20% over first
        quarter. Sales are up 30%.
        Stockholders' equity jumped by
        $400,000. The best news is the
        company's ratio of current assets to
        current liabilities. It is now 3.0,
        a full 1.0 higher than this time
        last year.

The raw maerial market remains stable, thanks
to a strong domestic supply. We have been told
to expect price reductions in materials over
the next two quarters. THis will enable us to
stabilize prices for our customers and realize
a larger profit.

                        K.J. Farnsworth
                        President

Move cursor; press Enter to retrieve.        Doc 1 Pg 1 Ln 4.67" Pos 2"
```

Move prompt

Now you must move the cursor to the location where you want to place the deleted paragraph and press the (Enter) key in order to retrieve the paragraph in this location. Move the cursor to the line before the third paragraph and press (Enter).

```
Current market conditions indicate that Trendy
Togs, Inc. will continue to build upon the
gains displayed in this 1991 second quarter
report.

        Profit climed 20% over first
        quarter. Sales are up 30%.
        Stockholders' equity jumped by
        $400,000. The best news is the
        company's ratio of current assets to
        current liabilities. It is now 3.0,
        a full 1.0 higher than this time
        last year.

The company recently purchased Baby Bottles, a
local designer diaper manufacturer. Baby
Bottles has been relatively stagnant over the
last five years, but we fully intend to
increase volume through Trendy Togs' strong
sales and distribution network within the next
year. This support, combined with Trendy Togs'
new line of designer baby clothes, should
increase the profitability of Baby Bottles
tremendously.
C:\QUARTER                              Doc 1 Pg 1 Ln 3.5" Pos 2"
```

Deleted paragraph appears in new location

The third and fourth paragraphs have switched locations in the document. To display both paragraphs, press the ⬇ key until you reach the end of the document. When using the Move feature, the text that is copied to the temporary buffer will remain there until new text is stored in the buffer or until you exit WordPerfect.

If, while the Move prompt is still displayed on the screen, you decide that you don't want to move the selected text, you can press Cancel (F1). This will remove the Move prompt from the screen. However, in order to retrieve the text, you must activate the Move feature again, select Retrieve and then select Block or simply activate Retrieve (Shift+F10) and press Enter. Remember that the text will be retrieved to the current cursor location.

Now let's save our document to retain the changes we've just made. Activate Save by pressing F10 or by selecting Save from the File menu with the keyboard or the mouse.

Checking for spelling errors

You should check your document for spelling errors before printing the document. WordPerfect's Speller feature checks your document not only for misspelled words but also for other common mistakes, such as capitalization errors.

The Speller also contains special options, such as counting the number of words in a document. With the Speller you can check a specific word, a page, an entire document or a block of text.

Now let's use the Speller to check our sample document.

Note:

The Speller files are needed in order to use this feature. If these files weren't installed when WordPerfect was installed, they must be installed now.

Activate the Speller by pressing [Ctrl]+[F2] or selecting Spell from the Tools menu with the keyboard or the mouse.

```
           last year.

The company recently purchased Baby Bottles, a
local designer diaper manufacturer. Baby
Bottles has been relatively stagnant over the
last five years, but we fully intend to
increase volume through Trendy Togs' strong
sales and distribution network within the next
year. This support, combined with Trendy Togs'
new line of designer baby clothes, should
increase the profitability of Baby Bottles
tremendously.

The raw maerial market remains stable, thanks
to a strong domestic supply. We have been told
to expect price reductions in materials over
the next two quarters. THis will enable us to
stabilize prices for our customers and realize
a larger profit.

                         K.J. Farnsworth
                         President

Check: 1 Word; 2 Page; 3 Document; 4 New Sup. Dictionary; 5 Look Up; 6 Count: 0
```

Activating the Speller

A menu appears in the status line at the bottom of the screen. The Word option checks the word on which the cursor is located. The

Page option checks the page in which the cursor is currently located. The Document option checks the entire document. The Supplementary Dictionary option enables you to switch to a different dictionary. (Refer to your WordPerfect manual for more information about this.) The Count option counts the number of words in the document.

Since we want to check our entire document, press the ③ or Ⓓ key to select the Document option.

When a misspelled word is found, it is highlighted and the normal editing screen will be divided into two sections. The top portion of the screen contains the text in the normal editing screen and the bottom portion contains a menu of options and various words that can be used to replace the misspelled word. The words that are displayed in the Speller screen are similar to the highlighted word either because of their spelling or their sound.

```
Current market conditions indicate that Trendy
Togs, Inc. will continue to build upon the
gains displayed in this 1991 second quarter
report.

        Profit climed 20% over first
        quarter. Sales are up 30%.
        Stockholders' equity jumped by
        $400,000. The best news is the
        company's ratio of current assets to
        current liabilities. It is now 3.0,
                                Doc 1 Pg 1 Ln 2.17" Pos 3.2"
 ^       ^     {   ^     ^     ^     ^     ^     ^     ^     }   ^     ^     ^     ^
  A. chimed              B. claimed              C. climbed
  D. clime               E. climes               F. limed
  G. clammed             H. climate



Not Found: 1 Skip Once; 2 Skip; 3 Add; 4 Edit; 5 Look Up; 6 Ignore Numbers: 0
```

The Speller screen

In our sample document, the word "climed" is highlighted. Obviously, this word should be "climbed".

There are several things you can do when Speller finds an error. You can either skip only this occurrence of the word, skip this and all occurrences of the word, add the word to a supplementary dictionary or correct the spelling of the word.

To replace an incorrect word in a document with one of the words listed by Speller, press the letter key that corresponds to the letter listed beside the appropriate word. For example, press Ⓒ to replace "climed" in our document with "climbed". Speller places "climbed" in our document and moves to the next misspelled word. Next, the word "maerial" is highlighted. Since this word should be "material", press the <A> key to replace the incorrect word. Again the corrected word is inserted in the document and Speller continues to check the document.

Next, the word "THis", in the last paragraph, is highlighted.

```
tremendously.

The raw material market remains stable, thanks
to a strong domestic supply. We have been told
to expect price reductions in materials over
the next two quarters. THis will enable us to
stabilize prices for our customers and realize
a larger profit.

                              K. J. Farnsworth
                              President
                                 Doc 1 Pg 1 Ln 6" Pos 4.3"
 ^     ^   {    ^     ^     ^     ^     ^     ^     ^  }   ^      ^     ^    ^

Irregular Case: 1 2 Skip; 3 Replace; 4 Edit; 5 Disable Case Checking
```

Capitalization error highlighted by Speller

Notice that Speller displays a different menu in status line. This menu is displayed when Speller encounters a capitalization error. The Skip and Edit options work the same as for misspelled words. The Replace option corrects capitalization according to a certain pattern (refer to your WordPerfect manual for details). The Disable Case Checking option will discontinue the checking of case in the rest of the document.

For our sample document, press ③ to correct the capitalization error. The "H" will be changed to lowercase.

Finally, Speller highlights "Farnsworth". Since this is a proper name, it doesn't need to be changed. So press the ② key to skip this word.

When the Speller is finished checking the document, it counts the number of words in the document. This number is displayed in the status line at the bottom of the screen.

```
tremendously.

The raw material market remains stable, thanks
to a strong domestic supply. We have been told
to expect price reductions in materials over
the next two quarters. This will enable us to
stabilize prices for our customers and realize
a larger profit.

                            K.J. Farnsworth
                            President




Word count: 166        Press any key to continue
```

Speller finished checking document

To exit the Speller, press any key; the normal status line will return.

It's very important to save your document after using the Speller so that you can retain the corrected version of your document.

Searching for and replacing text

Although the Speller feature checks and corrects words that have incorrect spellings or other mistakes, it cannot check whether the meaning of the word is correct. Sometimes a word may be spelled correctly but may not be the appropriate word to use in the document. These types of words can only be found by reading through your documents. Once you've done this, you can determine whether any words or phrases should be changed. For example, in our sample document, the word "bottles" was accidentally entered. This word should actually be "bottoms".

Instead of manually changing each occurrence of "bottles", we can use WordPerfect's Replace feature. To activate Replace, press Alt + F2 or select Replace from the Search menu with the keyboard or mouse.

```
tremendously.

The raw material market remains stable, thanks
to a strong domestic supply. We have been told
to expect price reductions in materials over
the next two quarters. This will enable us to
stabilize prices for our customers and realize
a larger profit.

                              K.J. Farnsworth
                              President













w/Confirm? No (Yes)
```

Activating Replace

In the status line a prompt, asking whether you want to confirm each replacement before it's made, appears. If "No" is selected, the replacements will automatically be made in the document. Press Ⓨ to switch on the confirmation.

```
tremendously.

The raw material market remains stable, thanks
to a strong domestic supply. We have been told
to expect price reductions in materials over
the next two quarters. This will enable us to
stabilize prices for our customers and realize
a larger profit.

                              K.J. Farnsworth
                                   President
```

`-> Srch:`

Setting the Search direction

The abbreviation `->  Srch` appears in the status line. Now you must select the direction of the search: either "down" (forward) from the current cursor position or "up" (backward) from the current cursor position. The default setting is "down".

Since the cursor is located at the end of our sample document, press the ⬆ key to search backward from the cursor. Notice that the arrow in the status line now points to the left.

Next, type the text that should be replaced, which is called the "search string". Type "bottles" and press Search (F2). The `Replace with:` prompt appears. Type the replacement text, "bottoms", and press Search (F2) again.

```
            a full 1.0 higher than this time
            last year.

       The company recently purchased Baby Bottles, a
       local designer diaper manufacturer. Baby
       Bottles has been relatively stagnant over the
       last five years, but we fully intend to
       increase volume through Trendy Togs' strong
       sales and distribution network within the next
       year. This support, combined with Trendy Togs'
       new line of designer baby clothes, should
       increase the profitability of Baby Bottles
       tremendously.

       The raw material market remains stable, thanks
       to a strong domestic supply. We have been told
       to expect price reductions in materials over
       the next two quarters. This will enable us to
       stabilize prices for our customers and realize
       a larger profit.

                             K.J. Farnsworth
                             President

<- Srch: Bottles
```

Starting the Search process

WordPerfect searches the document for the search string and when
"bottles" is found, the cursor stops at the word and the confirmation
prompt appears in the status line.

To replace the word with the replacement text "bottoms", press Y.

```
          Profit climbed 20% over first
          quarter. Sales are up 30%.
          Stockholders' equity jumped by
          $400,000. The best news is the
          company's ratio of current assets to
          current liabilities. It is now 3.0,
          a full 1.0 higher than this time
          last year.

     The company recently purchased Baby Bottles, a
     local designer diaper manufacturer. Baby
     Bottles has been relatively stagnant over the
     last five years, but we fully intend to
     increase volume through Trendy Togs' strong
     sales and distribution network within the next
     year. This support, combined with Trendy Togs'
     new line of designer baby clothes, should
     increase the profitability of Baby Bottoms
     tremendously.

     The raw material market remains stable, thanks
     to a strong domestic supply. We have been told
     to expect price reductions in materials over
     the next two quarters. This will enable us to
Confirm? No (Yes)                         Doc 1 Pg 1 Ln 4" Pos 2.1"
```

Replacement text is inserted

The word "bottoms" replaces "bottles" in the document. Continue to press the Ⓨ key until all occurrences of "bottles" have been changed to "bottoms". When the search and replace process is complete, WordPerfect automatically returns to the normal editing screen.

```
report.

        Profit climbed 20% over first
        quarter. Sales are up 30%.
        Stockholders' equity jumped by
        $400,000. The best news is the
        company's ratio of current assets to
        current liabilities. It is now 3.0,
        a full 1.0 higher than this time
        last year.

The company recently purchased Baby Bottoms, a
local designer diaper manufacturer. Baby
Bottoms has been relatively stagnant over the
last five years, but we fully intend to
increase volume through Trendy Togs' strong
sales and distribution network within the next
year. This support, combined with Trendy Togs'
new line of designer baby clothes, should
increase the profitability of Baby Bottoms
tremendously.

The raw material market remains stable, thanks
to a strong domestic supply. We have been told
```
C:\QUARTER   Doc 1 Pg 1 Ln 3.67" Pos 5.7"

Search and Replace completed

Notice that although we entered "bottles" and "bottoms" with a lowercase "b" in our search string and replacement text, the words found and the words inserted in the document have an uppercase "B". This occurs because lowercase letters in a search string or replacement text will match lower or uppercase letters in a document. However, if you enter uppercase letters in a search string, only uppercase letters will be matched in the document.

Before moving on to the next section, save your document by pressing (F10) or selecting Save from the File menu.

Using the Thesaurus

Another important aspect of editing a document is ensuring that the words that are used convey the proper meaning. Usually a thesaurus is used to find the appropriate word to use in a document. WordPerfect contains its own built-in thesaurus. So you can easily find synonyms and antonyms for the words in your documents or for words that you enter from the keyboard.

Now let's use the Thesaurus feature with our sample document.

Note: The Thesaurus file is needed in order to use this feature. If this file wasn't installed when WordPerfect was installed, it must be installed now.

Let's try to find a different word to use for "realize", which is located at the end of the last paragraph. First move the cursor to this word. Then activate the Thesaurus feature by pressing [Alt]+[F1] or selecting Thesaurus from the Tools menu with the keyboard or mouse.

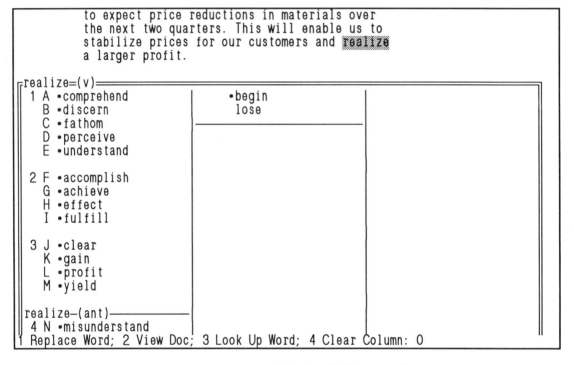

Activating the Thesaurus feature

When the Thesaurus is activated, the Thesaurus screen appears. This screen takes up most of the normal editing screen; only four lines from the normal editing screen are displayed. The word "realize" is highlighted in the document and a menu of options appears at the bottom of the screen.

The Thesaurus screen contains alternatives for the highlighted word in the document. In the first line of the screen, "realize" appears. This word is called a "headword", which is a word that can be looked up in the Thesaurus. The words listed under headwords are divided into nouns, verbs, adjectives and antonyms. These words are called references.

If a reference has a bullet (•) displayed in front of it, additional references can be displayed for this reference. References are divided into subgroups, which are numbered on the Thesaurus screen. All the words in a subgroup have similar meanings.

The Reference menu are the uppercase, bold letters that are located next to the words in the Thesaurus screen.

Now let's try looking up some words. As you'll see, there are several ways to do this.

One way to do this is to select the Look Up Word option from the menu at the bottom of the screen by pressing the ③ key. A prompt, asking for the word that you want to look up, appears. Type "fulfill" and press (Enter).

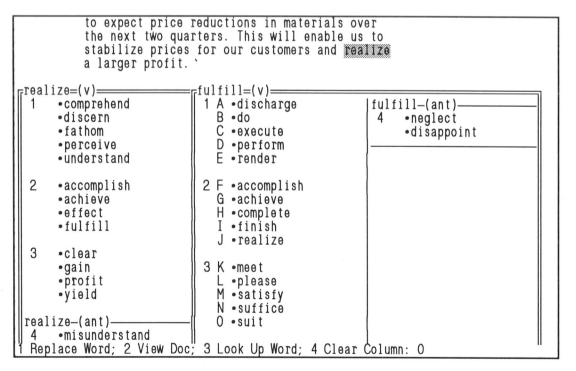

Using the Look Up Word option

The references for "fulfill" appear in the second and third columns. Notice that the Reference menu moved to the second column.

Since all the references for "fulfill" don't fit in one column, they are continued in the next column to the right. To display additional references, either press the ⬆ or ⬇ keys or move the Reference menu to the appropriate column.

Let's try this now. Press the ⬇ key. The second subgroup moves to the top of the Thesaurus screen and the third column adjusts accordingly. Then press the ⬆ key to return to the previous display.

Now press the ➡ key to move the Reference menu to the third column.

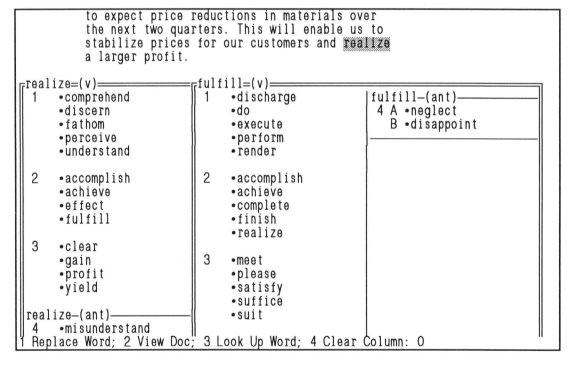

```
      to expect price reductions in materials over
      the next two quarters. This will enable us to
      stabilize prices for our customers and realize
      a larger profit.
┌realize=(v)════════════╦fulfill=(v)═══════════
││ 1    •comprehend      ║ 1    •discharge      ┌fulfill-(ant)──────────
││      •discern         ║      •do             │ 4 A •neglect
││      •fathom          ║      •execute        │   B •disappoint
││      •perceive        ║      •perform        │
││      •understand      ║      •render         │
││                       ║                      │
││ 2    •accomplish      ║ 2    •accomplish     │
││      •achieve         ║      •achieve        │
││      •effect          ║      •complete       │
││      •fulfill         ║      •finish         │
││                       ║      •realize        │
││ 3    •clear           ║                      │
││      •gain            ║ 3    •meet           │
││      •profit          ║      •please         │
││      •yield           ║      •satisfy        │
││                       ║      •suffice        │
│realize-(ant)─────────── ║      •suit          │
│ 4    •misunderstand    ║
 1 Replace Word; 2 View Doc; 3 Look Up Word; 4 Clear Column: 0
```

Moving the Reference menu

Then press the ⬅ key to move the menu back to the second column.

Another way to look up a word is to type the letter that appears next to a headword. For example, press the Ⓚ key to display references for the word "meet".

These references appear in the third column and the references for "fulfill" are moved to the second column. However, both of these columns contain additional references that are listed below the Thesaurus screen. To display these references, press the ⬇ key. Do this now. Continue to press this key until a solid horizontal line appears across the column. This line signifies the end of the references.

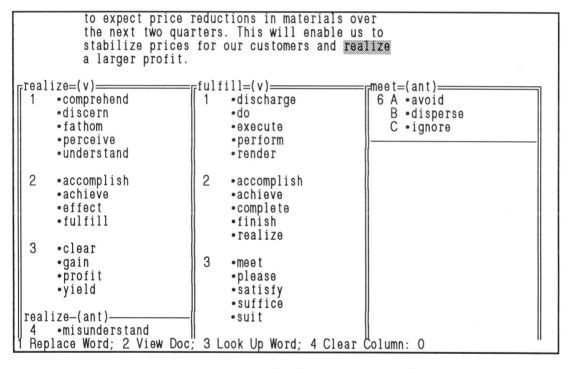

```
         to expect price reductions in materials over
         the next two quarters. This will enable us to
         stabilize prices for our customers and realize
         a larger profit.
┌realize=(v)════════════╤═fulfill=(v)══════════╤═meet=(ant)═══════════
│  1   •comprehend      │  1    •discharge     │  6 A •avoid
│      •discern         │       •do            │    B •disperse
│      •fathom          │       •execute       │    C •ignore
│      •perceive        │       •perform       │
│      •understand      │       •render        │
│                       │                      │
│  2   •accomplish      │  2    •accomplish    │
│      •achieve         │       •achieve       │
│      •effect          │       •complete      │
│      •fulfill         │       •finish        │
│                       │       •realize       │
│  3   •clear           │                      │
│      •gain            │  3    •meet          │
│      •profit          │       •please        │
│      •yield           │       •satisfy       │
│                       │       •suffice       │
│realize-(ant)──────────│       •suit          │
│  4   •misunderstand   │
│ Replace Word; 2 View Doc; 3 Look Up Word; 4 Clear Column: 0
```

Moving to the end of a column

You can also look up words by selecting the View Document option from the menu at the bottom of the screen, moving the cursor to another word in the document and then activating the Thesaurus feature again. The old references are cleared and the references for the new word appear.

The Clear Column option can be used to clear a column in the Thesaurus screen. The column in which the cursor is currently located will be affected. Let's clear the third column by pressing the ④ key. Then press the ④ key again to clear the second column.

The columns are cleared and the Reference menu returns to the first column. Now let's replace "realize" in our sample document with "achieve". To do this, select the Replace Word option by pressing ①. A prompt, asking for the appropriate letter, appears. Press the Ⓖ key.

```
to expect price reductions in materials over
the next two quarters. This will enable us to
stabilize prices for our customers and achieve
a larger profit.

                          K.J. Farnsworth
                          President
```

```
C:\QUARTER                        Doc 1 Pg 1 Ln 6.17" Pos 6.6"
```

Replacing a word in the document

The word "achieve" is inserted in the document and the Thesaurus screen is cleared. If, after activating the Thesaurus feature, you decide that you don't want to replace any words in your document, simply press Exit (F7) to return to the normal editing screen.

Once again, save your document by activating the Save feature (F10) or Save from the File menu).

Displaying your document	Once you've formatted and edited your document, it can be printed. However, before actually printing your documents, you can see how they will look when printed. The WordPerfect View Document feature displays, on the normal editing screen, how a document will look when it is printed.
Note:	This feature only works when the printer is selected.
	Let's use this feature now. Activate the Print feature by pressing [Shift]+[F7] or selecting Print from the File menu using the keyboard or the mouse. The Print menu will appear on your screen:

```
Print

     1 - Full Document
     2 - Page
     3 - Document on Disk
     4 - Control Printer
     5 - Multiple Pages
     6 - View Document
     7 - Initialize Printer


Options

     S - Select Printer
     B - Binding Offset                0"
     N - Number of Copies              1
     U - Multiple Copies Generated by  WordPerfect
     G - Graphics Quality              Medium
     T - Text Quality                  High




Selection: 0
```

Activating Print

From this menu, select the View Document option by pressing [6] or [V] or by clicking with the mouse.

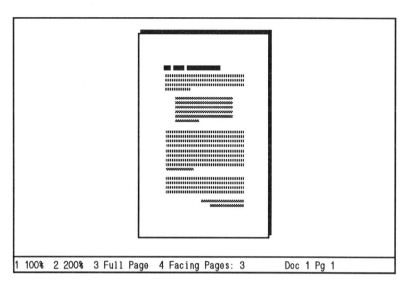

1 100%	2 200%	3 Full Page	4 Facing Pages: 3	Doc 1 Pg 1

View Document activated

Your document will appear on the screen as it will look when printed. The 100% option displays the document at its actual size, and the 200% option displays the document at twice its actual size. The Full Page option displays the entire page and the Facing Pages option displays two pages. Press Exit (F7) to exit this screen.

The following tables list the key combinations and menu options of commands discussed in this section.

Action	Key combination
Block	Alt + F4
Move	Ctrl + F4
Replace	Alt + F2
Retrieve file	Shift + F10
Speller	Ctrl + F2
Thesaurus	Alt + F1
View document	Shift + F7, 6
	Shift + F7, V

Action	Menu selection
Block	Edit/Block
Move	Edit/Move (Cut)
Replace	Search/Replace
Retrieve file	File/Retrieve
Speller	Tools/Spell
Thesaurus	Tools/Thesaurus
View document	File/Print/view document

4.4 Advanced Formatting Features

In this section you'll create a new document and learn how to use some of WordPerfect's more advanced formatting features. After working through the previous sections, you should have a good idea of how many of the WordPerfect features and options work. This will make it easier for you to work with the features we'll present in this section.

Before we get started, we must save the sample document, QUARTER, and clear the screen so we can create a new document. To do this, activate Exit by pressing `F7` or by selecting Exit from the File menu with the keyboard or mouse. Answer "Yes" to the Save document? prompt by pressing the `Y` key and then press `Enter` when the filename appears in the status line. Then press `Y` to save the most recent version of the document and press `N` to clear the screen and remain in WordPerfect.

In this section we'll create a balance sheet for our imaginary company, Trendy Togs, Inc. First enter the following lines, exactly as they appear below. After the first and second lines, press the `Enter` key once and after the third line press the `Enter` key twice.

```
TRENDY TOGS, INCORPORATED
Balance Sheet
(unaudited)

ASSETS
```

Centering lines

You may remember that earlier in this chapter we centered our sample document between the top and bottom margins by using the Center Page option from the Format Page submenu. It's also possible to center individual lines within your document by using WordPerfect's Center feature.

Let's try using this feature now. First move the cursor, with the arrow keys, to the beginning of the first line. When using this feature it's very important that the cursor is located at the very beginning of the line you want to center. If the cursor isn't in this location, the text may not be centered properly. For our example, you can ensure that the cursor is located at the beginning of the line by the numbers listed in the status line. The line number and cursor position number should both be "1"".

Now activate the Center feature by pressing (Shift)+(F6) or selecting Align from the Layout menu and then selecting Center using the keyboard or the mouse. Then press the (↓) key. Your screen should look similar to the following:

```
                         TRENDY TOGS, INCORPORATED
Balance Sheet
(unaudited)

ASSETS




























                                        Doc 1 Pg 1 Ln 1.17" Pos 2.3"
```

Activating the Center feature

Although the line doesn't look centered on your screen, it will be located in the center of the page when the document is printed. Now let's center the second and third lines. However, instead of the method we just used, we'll try another method WordPerfect provides for centering lines.

This time we'll use the Center Justification feature. The difference between these features is that the Center feature is designed for centering individual lines of text and the Center Justification feature is designed for centering multiple lines of text. The Center feature inserts a code that is switched off at the end of a line (at the Hard return code). So in order to use this feature to center several lines of text, you must insert a center code (activate the Center feature) at the beginning of every line that should be centered. As you will see, it is much faster to use the Center Justification feature instead.

The Center Justification feature is one of the many WordPerfect features that can be used with the Block feature. So the second and third lines of our sample balance sheet must be "blocked". First move the cursor to the beginning of the second line (to the "B" of Balance sheet). Then activate the Block feature by pressing `Alt`+`F4` or selecting Block from the Edit menu with the keyboard or mouse. When the "Block on" message begins to flash in the status line, press the `→` key until both lines are highlighted.

Now activate the Center feature by pressing `Shift`+`F6` or selecting Align from the Layout menu and then selecting Center with the keyboard or mouse.

```
                        TRENDY TOGS, INCORPORATED
Balance Sheet
(unaudited)

ASSETS

















[Just:Center]? No (Yes)
```

Using Center with the Block feature

109

A prompt, asking you whether the lines should be set to Center Justification, appears in the status line. Press the Ⓨ key to select this justification. As you can see, both lines are centered on your screen.

Since we used the same feature in both of the previous examples, you may be wondering why the methods are considered different. To understand why this is so, let's activate the Reveal Codes screen by pressing Alt+F3 or by selecting Reveal Codes from the Edit menu using the keyboard or the mouse.

```
                   TRENDY TOGS, INCORPORATED
                        Balance Sheet
                        (unaudited)

ASSETS




C:\BALANCE                                      Doc 1 Pg 1 Ln 1.5" Pos 1"
{        ^    ^    ^   ^   ^    ^       ^     _                }  ^     ^
[Center]TRENDY TOGS, INCORPORATED[HRt]
[Just:Center]Balance Sheet[HRt]
(unaudited)[HRt]
[Just:Full][HRt]
ASSETS




Press Reveal Codes to restore screen
```

Displaying codes

As you can see, a Center code was placed before the first line of our document. Since the Center feature only applies to one line at a time, it is switched off when it encounters a Hard return code. So a Center Off code doesn't appear in the Reveal Codes screen. Now let's look at the code that was inserted before the second line of our document. Instead of a Center code, a Justification Center code was inserted in this location. As we learned earlier in this chapter, when a Justification code is switched off, it returns the Justification back to the original setting. So in our document, the Justification Full code, which is the default setting, is inserted after the second line.

To switch off the Reveal Codes screen, press [Alt]+[F3] again or select Reveal Codes from the Edit menu using the keyboard or mouse. Now let's save our document. To do this either press [F10] or select Save from the File menu using the keyboard or mouse. Type the filename BALANCE after the Document to be saved: prompt and press [Enter]. The filename will now appear in the status line.

Changing fonts

In this section we'll change the font that will be used in the rest of our document. We can make this change by using the Base Font option. Before using this option, let's briefly discuss what a base font is.

When you select the printer you will use with WordPerfect, a base font is assigned to the printer. This font is used as the basis for the normal text in your documents. Normal text is text that doesn't contain any attributes. Any text attributes, such as Bold and Italic, that you select for your documents are usually variations of the base font. However, this often depends on the number of fonts that are available on your printer.

Note:

For more information on base fonts and printer selection, refer to your WordPerfect manual. The list of fonts that WordPerfect will display depends on the installed printer that is currently selected.

The Base Font option enables you to change the font used in your document. This option inserts a code that changes the font from the code through the entire document. Let's try using this option now. First ensure that the cursor is located in the line above "ASSETS". Then activate the Font feature by pressing [Ctrl]+[F8] and then select the Base Font option by pressing [4] or [F]. To use the pull-down menus, simply select Base Font from the Font menu with the keyboard or the mouse.

The following font list is for a PostScript compatible printer; your font list may differ.

```
Base Font

* Courier
  Courier Bold
  Courier Bold Oblique
  Courier Oblique
  Helvetica
  Helvetica Bold
  Helvetica Bold Oblique
  Helvetica Narrow
  Helvetica Narrow Bold
  Helvetica Narrow Bold Oblique
  Helvetica Narrow Oblique
  Helvetica Oblique
  ITC Avant Garde Gothic Book
  ITC Avant Garde Gothic Book Oblique
  ITC Avant Garde Gothic Demi
  ITC Avant Garde Gothic Demi Oblique
  ITC Bookman Demi
  ITC Bookman Demi Italic
  ITC Bookman Light
  ITC Bookman Light Italic
  ITC Zapf Chancery Medium Italic

1 Select; N Name search: 1
```

Base Font screen

A list of available fonts will appear on the screen. Most printers will have a "Courier" monospaced font available. This font is similar to the one that is produced by most typewriters. Select a "Courier" font by moving the cursor to this font and activating Select by pressing ⑤ or ①.

WordPerfect prompts for a point size when using a Postscript compatible printer. Enter 12 and press (Enter). If you're using a dot matrix printer you can select the point size when you select the font. Dot matrix printer users should select a Courier 10cpi (characters per inch) font.

Although the appearance of the text on the screen won't change to reflect the new font setting, a code has been inserted in your document. This code indicates that the selected font should be used for rest of the document. This font will remain in effect for the entire document unless the base font is changed again.

Let's display this code by activating Reveal Codes by pressing `Alt`+`F3` or selecting Reveal Codes from the Edit menu with the keyboard or the mouse.

```
                      TRENDY TOGS, INCORPORATED
                            Balance Sheet
                             (unaudited)
ASSETS




C:\BALANCE                                  Doc 1 Pg 1 Ln 1.67" Pos 1.6"
{    ^     ^    ^    ^    ^   ^    ^    ^       ^   ^    ^   }    ^    ^
[Just:Center]Balance Sheet[HRt]
(unaudited)[HRt]
[Just:Full][Font:Courier 12pt][HRt]
ASSETS




Press Reveal Codes to restore screen
```

Displaying the Base Font code

To save the changes you've just made, activate Save by pressing `F10` or by selecting Save from the File menu with the keyboard or mouse.

Drawing lines

With the WordPerfect Graphic feature you can insert various types of graphics in your documents. This feature enables you to do many things. For example, you can create several types of graphics boxes. These boxes can be inserted into a document and text can be placed around them. It's also possible to place graphics, text or equations in these boxes.

The Graphics feature can also be used to draw lines in your document. Let's try doing this now in our document. First move the cursor to the "A" of "ASSETS". Activate the Graphics feature by pressing `Alt`+`F9` and selecting the Line option by pressing `5` or `L`.

```
TRENDY TOGS, INCORPORATED
      Balance Sheet
       (unaudited)

ASSETS
```

Create Line: 1 Horizontal; 2 Vertical; Edit Line: 3 Horizontal; 4 Vertical: 0

The Graphics Line submenu

In the menu that appears, select the Horizontal option by pressing the
1 or H key.

To use the pull-down menus, select Line from the Graphics menu and
then select the Create Horizontal option with the keyboard or mouse.

```
┌─────────────────────────────────────────────────────────────────┐
│Graphics: Horizontal Line                                         │
│                                                                   │
│    1 - Horizontal Position      Full                              │
│                                                                   │
│    2 - Vertical Position        Baseline                          │
│                                                                   │
│    3 - Length of Line                                             │
│                                                                   │
│    4 - Width of Line            0.013"                            │
│                                                                   │
│    5 - Gray Shading (% of black) 100%                             │
│                                                                   │
│                                                                   │
│                                                                   │
│                                                                   │
│                                                                   │
│                                                                   │
│                                                                   │
│                                                                   │
│                                                                   │
│                                                                   │
│Selection: 0                                                       │
└─────────────────────────────────────────────────────────────────┘
```

The Graphics Horizontal Line submenu

As you can see, the Graphics Horizontal Line submenu appears on your screen. The options in this menu enable you to adjust how the horizontal line will appear in your document.

First let's select the Horizontal Position option by pressing the ⬚1⬚ or ⬚H⬚ key or clicking on the option with the mouse. A menu appears in the status line at the bottom of the screen. The setting selected in this menu will determine how your line will be positioned on the page. If you select Left or Right, the line will be positioned to one of these margins. Selecting Center will center the line between the margins and selecting Full will extend the line from the left to right margin. You can also position the line to the current cursor position by selecting Set Position.

For our document, we'll use the Full setting, which is the default setting. Press Cancel (⬚F1⬚) to return to the submenu. The next option, Vertical Position, allows you to set the height for the area between the bottom of the line and the text line below it. Activate this option now by pressing ⬚2⬚ or ⬚V⬚ or clicking with the mouse. The

115

default setting for this option is Baseline, which aligns the bottom of the horizontal line with the baseline of the line from with the graphics line setting is made. The baseline is the line on which the characters are placed. If you don't want your graphic line to be aligned with a text line's baseline, you can use the Set Position setting to determine the distance from the top of the page. Again we'll use the default setting; so press Cancel (F1) to return to the submenu.

The third option in the Graphics Horizontal Line submenu is Length of Line. You can use this option to indicate the length of the line. However, notice that a setting doesn't appear for this option. If you press the 3 or L key or click with the mouse to select this option, nothing will happen. This setting cannot be changed when the Horizontal Position is set to "Full", which is the case for our document.

The Width of Line option lets you set the thickness of the line. If you increase the width, the direction in which the line expands depends on the setting made in the Vertical Position option. If Baseline is used, the line expands up and if Set Position is used, the line expands down. Again we'll use the default setting for this option.

Gray Shading is the last option in this submenu. This option allows you to set the amount of black that will be used in the shading of the line. Select this option by pressing 5 or G or clicking with the mouse and type "50%". When you press Enter, this setting will be displayed in the menu. Now press Enter again to return to the normal editing screen.

Although WordPerfect doesn't display the line on the screen, a code is inserted in the document and the line will appear when the document is printed. To display the code that was inserted in the document, activate Reveal Codes (Alt+F3) or select Reveal Codes from the Edit menu with the keyboard or mouse).

```
┌──────────────────────────────────────────────────────────────────────────┐
│                    TRENDY TOGS, INCORPORATED                               │
│                        Balance Sheet                                       │
│                        (unaudited)                                         │
│ASSETS                                                                      │
│                                                                            │
│                                                                            │
│                                                                            │
│                                                                            │
│C:\BALANCE                                      Doc 1 Pg 1 Ln 1.67" Pos 1"  │
│{   ^    ^     ^      ^      ^     ^    ^    ^      ^   ^   ^         ^   ^   │
│[Just:Center]Balance Sheet[HRt]                                     }       │
│(unaudited)[HRt]                                                            │
│[Just:Full][HRt]                                                            │
│[HLine:Full,Baseline,6.5",0.013",50%]ASSETS                                 │
│                                                                            │
│                                                                            │
│                                                                            │
│                                                                            │
│                                                                            │
│Press Reveal Codes to restore screen                                        │
└──────────────────────────────────────────────────────────────────────────┘
```

Displaying the Horizontal Line code

As you can see, the Horizontal Line code appears before "ASSETS" in the Reveal Codes screen. Notice that the settings from the Graphics Horizontal Line submenu are also listed. To return to the normal editing screen, activate Reveal Codes again.

Setting tabs

If you've ever used a typewriter or another type of word processor, you're probably familiar with tabs. By using tabs, you can indent text a certain amount of space in a document. Tabs are very useful when you're working with rows and columns of information because they can quickly and efficiently align the text. If you don't use tabs in these instances, it would be very time-consuming to keep the spacing consistent between the items.

WordPerfect contains a standard set of tabs, which are automatically set when you begin a document. Each of these tabs are a half inch apart from each other. So, it's possible to insert a tab in a document by simply pressing the Tab key. This key is usually located in the upper-left portion of your keyboard and is identified with the letters "Tab" and/or arrows pointing left and right.

117

These tab settings are represented in the Reveal Codes screen as triangles:

```
                    TRENDY TOGS, INCORPORATED
                          Balance Sheet
                           (unaudited)

ASSETS




C:\BALANCE                                        Doc 1 Pg 1 Ln 1.67" Pos 1.6"
{      ^     ^      ^      ^     ^      ^      ^       ^    ^     ^    }    ^      ^
[Just:Center]Balance Sheet[HRt]
(unaudited)[HRt]
[Just:Full][HRt]
[HLine:Full,Baseline,6.5",0.013",50%]ASSETS





Press Reveal Codes to restore screen
```

Displaying the tab settings

However, you don't always have to use these standard tab settings. WordPerfect allows you to create your own tab settings and use different types of tabs depending on how you want to align your text. Now let's create some tabs for our sample document. Since this is a balance sheet, we will be entering two columns of numbers. As you'll see, using tabs will make creating this document much easier.

First ensure that the cursor is located after "ASSETS" and then press the (Enter) key twice. Now activate the Format feature by pressing (Shift)+(F8) and then select the Line option by pressing (1) or (L). To use the pull-down menus, select Line from the Layout menu using the keyboard or the mouse. The Format Line submenu should appear on your screen.

In order to set tabs, we must use the Tab Set option from this menu. Activate this option now by pressing the Ⓔ or Ⓣ key or clicking with the mouse. You should see the following on your screen:

```
                        TRENDY TOGS, INCORPORATED
                            Balance Sheet
                            (unaudited)

ASSETS












L....L....L....L....L....L....L....L....L....L....L....L....L....L....L....L...
|    ^    |    ^    |    ^    |    ^    |    ^    |    ^    |    ^    |    ^
0"        +1"       +2"       +3"       +4"       +5"       +6"       +7"
Delete EOL (clear tabs); Enter Number (set tab); Del (clear tab);
Type; Left; Center; Right; Decimal; .= Dot Leader; Press Exit when done.
```

Activating Tab Set

The Tab Set menu appears at the bottom of your screen. The first line, which is called the tab set line, contains the current tab settings. An "L" is displayed at each tab. This represents the Left type tab, which is the type of setting that is used for WordPerfect's standard tabs. The numbers that appear below the tab set line are the current line measurements. WordPerfect uses inches as the standard unit of measurement unless you change this setting by using the Setup feature. The third line displays the instructions for deleting and setting tabs. The last line in this menu displays the different types of tabs that can be selected.

First we'll delete the standard settings so that the only tabs in the document will be the ones we set. Deleting the standard tab settings can save you time because you won't have to press the ⌨Tab key repeatedly to pass unnecessary tab settings in order to reach the

119

desired tab setting. Before clearing all the tabs on the tab set line, first press the ⌐Home⌐ key twice and then press the ⊖ key. This moves the cursor to the very beginning of the tab set line. It's important to press these keys before deleting the tabs because the entire tab set line may not be visible on your screen. Press these keys now.

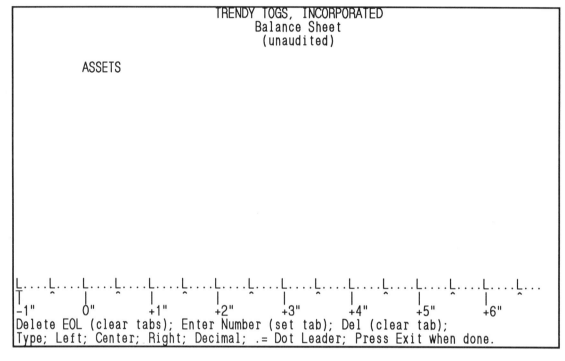

Moving the cursor to the beginning of the tab set line

As you can see, the cursor has moved to the very beginning of this line, which previously wasn't displayed on the screen. Now we're ready to delete the tab settings. To do this, press Delete to End of Line (⌐Ctrl⌐+⌐End⌐).

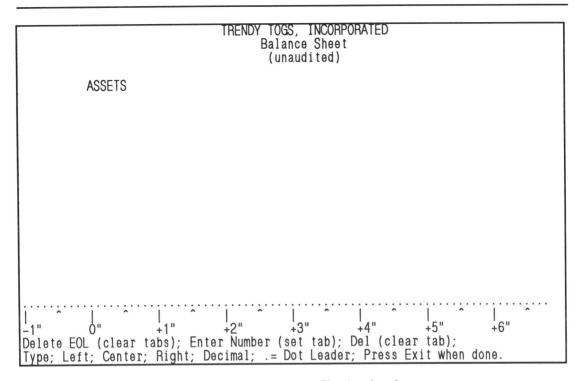

Clearing the tabs

As you can see, all the tabs are deleted from the current cursor position to the end of the tab set line. Now we're ready to set our own tabs. As we previously mentioned, WordPerfect allows you to select different types of tabs. There are four different types of tabs: Left, Center, Right and Decimal. Depending on which setting is selected, the text will be aligned at the tab stop (Left), centered over the tab setting (Center), aligned to the right at the tab stop (Right) or aligned at the align character (e.g., a decimal point) (Decimal).

Note:
For more information about the different types of tabs, refer to your WordPerfect manual.

To set tabs you must move the cursor, with the arrow keys, to the location where you want the tab. Let's set our first tab. Move the cursor, with the ➡ key to the "^" symbol between 0" and +1" and press Ⓛ. An uppercase "L" will appear on the tab set line above this location. A left tab is now inserted at this location. Next move the cursor to the "^" symbol between +1" and +2" and press Ⓛ to insert another left tab. Your screen should look similar to the following:

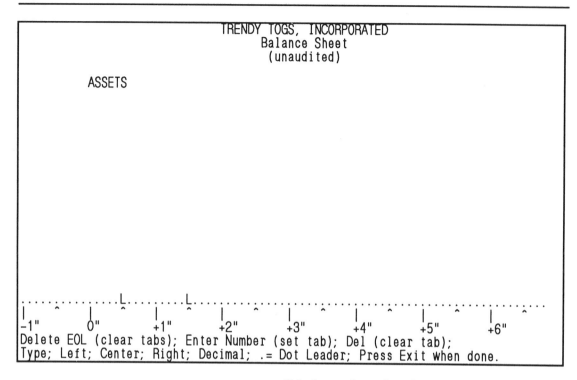

```
                         TRENDY TOGS, INCORPORATED
                             Balance Sheet
                             (unaudited)

        ASSETS
```

```
. . . . . . . . . . . . . . . .L. . . . . . . . . . .L. . . . . . . . . . . . . . . . . . . . . . . . . . . . . . . . . . . . . . . . . . . .
    ^         |         ^         |         ^         |         ^         |         ^         |         ^
|         |         |         |         |         |         |         |         |         |
-1"       0"        +1"       +2"       +3"       +4"       +5"       +6"
Delete EOL (clear tabs); Enter Number (set tab); Del (clear tab);
Type; Left; Center; Right; Decimal; .= Dot Leader; Press Exit when done.
```

Tabs inserted on tab set line

Now move the cursor to the point after the "^" symbol between +4" and +5" and press the Ⓡ key. This inserts a right tab at the cursor location. Then move the cursor to the point before the "^" symbol between +5" and +6" and press Ⓡ. To set our last tab, move the cursor to +6" and press Ⓡ. The text entered at these tab stops will be aligned from right to left (similar to the Flush Right feature). Your tab set line should look similar to the following:

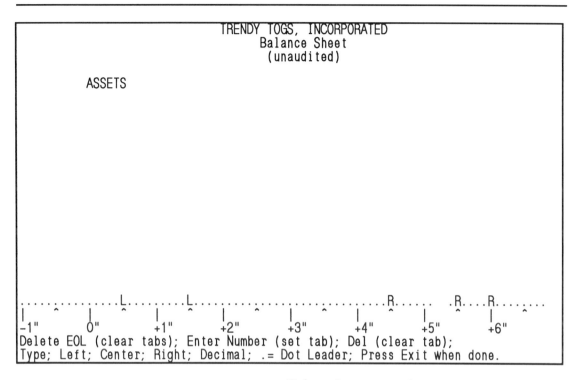

TRENDY TOGS, INCORPORATED
Balance Sheet
(unaudited)

ASSETS

```
..............L.........L....................................R...... .R...R........
|    ^     |         |         |         ^    |        ^   |       ^   |        ^
|-1"       0"        +1"       +2"       +3"       +4"       +5"       +6"
Delete EOL (clear tabs); Enter Number (set tab); Del (clear tab);
Type; Left; Center; Right; Decimal; .= Dot Leader; Press Exit when done.
```

Tabs settings are complete

Press Exit ([F7]) until you return to the normal editing screen. Now you can use the tabs by pressing the [Tab] key, which moves the cursor to each tab stop. Since our tab settings are established, we can enter the rest of the information for our balance sheet. Your cursor should still be located two lines below "ASSETS". At this location, press the [Tab] key four times and type "June 30". Notice that when you type in this text it will be aligned to the right instead of the left. Then press [Enter] and press the [Tab] key three times; type "1991". Now press the [Tab] key twice and type "1990"; press [Enter]. Your screen should look similar to the following:

```
                    TRENDY TOGS, INCORPORATED
                        Balance Sheet
                        (unaudited)

ASSETS

                                         June 30
                                   1991           1990
```
```
C:\BALANCE                            Doc 1 Pg 1 Ln 2.33" Pos 1"
```

Entering text at the tab stops

Note: The tab settings given here may not work correctly with your system. Tab settings can vary with each printer driver. If the illustrations below do not match your screen, you may have to experiment with tab settings.

At the current cursor location, enter "Current Assets:" and then press ⟨Enter⟩. Now do the following: press the ⟨Tab⟩ key once and type "Cash", press the ⟨Tab⟩ key twice and type "60,000", press the ⟨Tab⟩ key twice and type "30,000", press the ⟨Enter⟩ key.

Next, press the ⟨Tab⟩ key once and type "Accounts Receivable". Press the ⟨Tab⟩ key twice and type "600,000". Then press the ⟨Tab⟩ key twice and type "250,000". Press the ⟨Enter⟩ key when you're finished. Repeat this process until the following information is entered:

```
Inventory           350,000         350,000
Prepaid Expenses    80,000          35,000
```

Once this information is entered, your screen should look similar to the following:

```
                    TRENDY TOGS, INCORPORATED
                         Balance Sheet
                          (unaudited)

ASSETS

                                       June 30
                                1991              1990
Current Assets:
    Cash                        60,000            30,000
    Accounts Receivable        600,000           250,000
    Inventory                  350,000           350,000
    Prepaid Expenses            80,000            35,000










C:\BALANCE                              Doc 1 Pg 1 Ln 3.17" Pos 1"
```

Entering columns of numbers

Now press the ⬚Tab⬚ key twice and type "Total Current Assets", press the ⬚Tab⬚ key once and type "1,090,000". Then press the ⬚Tab⬚ key twice and type "665,000"; press ⬚Enter⬚. To enter the remaining information, use the procedure previously listed (for Cash, Accounts Receivable, etc.):

```
Property and Equipment   1,400,000    1,120,000
Other Assets                70,000       45,000
                         2,560,000    1,830,000
```

When you're finished, your screen should look similar to the following:

```
┌────────────────────────────────────────────────────────────────────────┐
│                    TRENDY TOGS, INCORPORATED                             │
│                       Balance Sheet                                      │
│                        (unaudited)                                       │
│                                                                          │
│ASSETS                                                                    │
│                                                                          │
│                                          June 30                         │
│                                       1991        1990                   │
│Current Assets:                                                           │
│   Cash                               60,000      30,000                  │
│   Accounts Receivable               600,000     250,000                  │
│   Inventory                         350,000     350,000                  │
│   Prepaid Expenses                   80,000      35,000                  │
│            Total Current Assets   1,090,000     665,000                  │
│   Property and Equipment          1,400,000   1,120,00                   │
│   Other Assets                       70,000      45,000                  │
│                                   2,560,000   1,830,000                  │
│                                                                          │
│                                                                          │
│                                                                          │
│                                                                          │
│                                                                          │
│                                                                          │
│C:\BALANCE                             Doc 1 Pg 1 Ln 3.83" Pos 1"         │
└────────────────────────────────────────────────────────────────────────┘
```

Completed balance sheet

Each time you press the Tab key a code is inserted in your document. To display these codes, activate Reveal Codes by pressing Alt + F3 or selecting Reveal Codes from the menu with the keyboard or the mouse. As you can see, left tabs are indicated by the [Tab] code and right tabs are indicated by the [Rgt Tab] code. Activate Reveal Codes again to return to the normal editing screen.

Note: It's possible to display a tab ruler at all times on your screen. Refer to Windows in your WordPerfect manual for details.

We're now finished entering information in our balance sheet. To save the changes you've made, activate the Save feature by pressing F10 or selecting Save from the File menu and press Enter and Y.

Underlining text   In this section we'll make some final formatting settings for our sample balance sheet. The columns of numbers we've created using tabs is difficult to read because nothing sets the numbers apart. For this reason, we need to underline the date, years and totals and then double underline the grand totals of the balance sheet.

To do this, first move the cursor to the "J" of "June" and activate the Block feature by pressing `Alt`+`F4` or selecting Block from the Edit menu. Then, using the `→` key, select this entire line. Once it's selected, activate the Underline feature by pressing `F8` or by selecting Appearance from the Font menu and then selecting Underline with the keyboard or mouse.

```
                     TRENDY TOGS, INCORPORATED
                         Balance Sheet
                          (unaudited)

ASSETS

                                          June 30
                                  1991              1990
Current Assets:
    Cash                          60,000            30,000
    Accounts Receivable          600,000           250,000
    Inventory                    350,000           350,000
    Prepaid Expenses              80,000            35,000
            Total Current Assets 1,090,000         665,000
    Property and Equipment       1,400,000         1,120,00
    Other Assets                  70,000            45,000
                                 2,560,000         1,830,000




C:\BALANCE                              Doc 1 Pg 1 Ln 2" Pos 6.4"
```

Activating the Underline feature

The line appears in reverse video on the screen. Although the line doesn't appear on the screen, it will be inserted when the document is printed. Activate Reveal Codes (`Alt`+`F3`) to display the Underline code. Notice that an on and off code were inserted before and after the line.

127

```
┌─────────────────────────────────────────────────────────────────────┐
│                    TRENDY TOGS, INCORPORATED                          │
│                        Balance Sheet                                  │
│                         (unaudited)                                   │
│                                                                       │
│ASSETS                                                                 │
│                                                                       │
│                                               June 30                 │
│                                        1991            1990           │
│Current Assets:                                                        │
│    Cash                                60,000          30,000         │
│    Accounts Receivable                600,000         250,000         │
│C:\BALANCE                                    Doc 1 Pg 1 Ln 2" Pos 6.4"│
│[                                             ]                        │
│[Just:Full][HRt]                                                       │
│[HLine:Full,Baseline,6.5",0.013",50%]ASSETS[HRt]                       │
│[HRt]                                                                  │
│[Tab Set:Rel; +0.5",+1.5",+4.6",+5.4",+6"][Tab][Tab][Rgt Tab][Rgt Tab][UND]June│
│30[und][HRt]                                                           │
│[Tab][Tab][Rgt Tab]1991[Rgt Tab][Rgt Tab]1990[HRt]                     │
│Current Assets:[HRt]                                                   │
│[Tab]Cash[Tab][Rgt Tab]60,000[Rgt Tab][Rgt Tab]30,000[HRt]            │
│[Tab]Accounts Receivable[Rgt Tab]600,000[Rgt Tab][Rgt Tab]250,000[HRt]│
│[Tab]Inventory[Tab][Rgt Tab]350,000[Rgt Tab][Rgt Tab]350,000[HRt]     │
│                                                                       │
│Press Reveal Codes to restore screen                                   │
└─────────────────────────────────────────────────────────────────────┘
```

Displaying the Underline codes

To return to the normal editing screen, activate Reveal Codes again. Now we'll underline the years 1991 and 1990. To do this, move the cursor to the "1" of 1991 and activate the Block feature. Select the line and then activate the Underline Feature ([F8] or select Appearance from the Font menu and then select Underline). Now this line appears in reverse video.

Repeat this process for the line containing the "80,000" and the "35,000" and the line containing "70,000" and "45,000". When you're finished, your screen should look similar to the following:

```
ASSETS

                                     June 30
                                  1991        1990
Current Assets:
    Cash                        60,000        30,000
    Accounts Receivable        600,000       250,000
    Inventory                  350,000       350,000
    Prepaid Expenses            80,000        35,000
            Total Current Assets 1,090,000    665,000
    Property and Equipment   1,400,000     1,120,00
    Other Assets                70,000        45,000
                             2,560,000     1,830,000




C:\BALANCE                          Doc 1 Pg 1 Ln 3.5" Pos 7"
```

Underlining text

Now we'll double underline the grand totals, which are the figures in the last row of the balance sheet. To do this, move the cursor to the "2" in the last line of the document and activate Block by pressing Alt + F4 or selecting Block from the Edit menu. Select the entire line and then select the Font feature by pressing Ctrl + F8. In the menu that appears, select Appearance by pressing 2 or A and then select Double Underline by pressing 3 or D. To use the pull-down menus, select Appearance from the Font menu and then select Double Underline by using the keyboard or mouse.

Again the lines will not appear on the screen but Double Underline codes will appear inserted in the document.

Our balance sheet is now complete so you should save it by activating Save (F10) or select Save from the File menu with the keyboard or mouse).

129

Switching between documents

Suppose that while you're working on the balance sheet we just completed, you also wanted to work on the letter to the shareholders, which we created earlier in this chapter. With WordPerfect, it's possible to switch between two documents in memory by using the Switch feature. This enables you to work with two different documents at the same time.

Let's try using this feature now. Activate Switch by pressing Shift + F3 or by selecting Switch Document from the Edit menu with the keyboard or the mouse. A clear editing screen should appear:

Doc 2 Pg 1 Ln 1" Pos 1"

Activating Switch

Although this looks like the usual screen that appears when WordPerfect starts, there is a difference. Notice that in the status line, a "2" appears after "Doc". This indicates that you are in the Document 2 screen. Now you can retrieve the document, Quarter, by activating the Retrieve feature (Shift + F10) or by selecting Retrieve from the File menu with the keyboard or the mouse) and entering "Quarter" in the line that appears. The document will appear on your screen; notice that the document number in the status line remains at "2".

To switch between the balance sheet document and this document, activate Switch ([Shift]+[F3] or select Switch Document from the Edit menu). The balance sheet will appear on your screen again.

In order to exit both of these documents, press Exit ([F7] or select Exit from the File menu). Save the balance sheet by pressing [Y], pressing [Enter] and pressing [Y]. The following prompt should appear:

```
                    TRENDY TOGS, INCORPORATED
                          Balance Sheet
                          (unaudited)

ASSETS

                                        June 30
                                    1991          1990
Current Assets:
    Cash                           60,000        30,000
    Accounts Receivable           600,000       250,000
    Inventory                     350,000       350,000
    Prepaid Expenses               80,000        35,000
               Total Current Assets 1,090,000   665,000
    Property and Equipment      1,400,000     1,120,00
    Other Assets                   70,000        45,000
                                2,560,000     1,830,000




Exit doc 1? No (Yes)                (Cancel to return to document)
```

Exiting the first document

At this point, you can either select "No" to clear the current screen but remain in WordPerfect or select "Yes" to close the current screen and switch to the other active document. Let's select "Yes" by pressing [Y]. The second document will appear on the screen. Now exit this document by activating Exit again. Save the document and remain in WordPerfect.

As you can see, "Doc 2" still appears in the status line. If there isn't a document in this screen, it will automatically be closed when you exit the WordPerfect program. To switch to document 1, activate Switch by pressing `Shift`+`F3` or selecting Switch Document from the Edit menu.

Creating a letterhead

In this section we'll create a letterhead for our imaginary company, Trendy Togs, Incorporated. This letterhead can be used on all the company's correspondence. To do this we'll be using the Header option from the Format feature and the Figure option from the Graphics feature.

Headers

To create a header for the letterhead, first activate the Format feature by pressing `Shift`+`F8` and selecting the Page option by pressing `2` or `P` or selecting Page from the Layout menu with the keyboard or the mouse. The Format Page menu will appear on your screen:

```
Format: Page

    1 - Center Page (top to bottom)      No

    2 - Force Odd/Even Page

    3 - Headers

    4 - Footers

    5 - Margins - Top                    1"
                  Bottom                 1"

    6 - Page Numbering

    7 - Paper Size                       8.5" x 11"
             Type                        Standard

    8 - Suppress (this page only)




Selection: 0
```

Activating Format Page

From this menu, select the Headers option by pressing ③ or Ⓗ. A menu will appear in the status line at the bottom of the screen. Press Ⓐ or ① to select the Header A option. Another menu will appear in the status line. Select the Every Page option by pressing ② or Ⓟ. The following should appear on the screen:

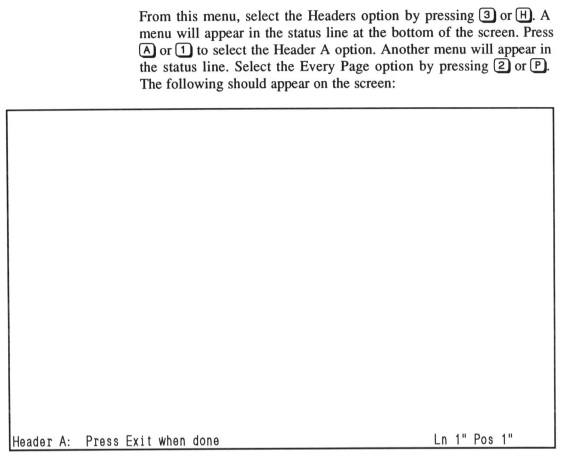

Creating a header

This is a special editing screen that is used to create headers and footers. You can use this screen the same way you've been using the normal editing screen. You can enter, edit and format text in the same way.

Now let's activate the Font feature by pressing Ctrl+F8. Then select the Size option by pressing ① or Ⓢ and select the Very Large option by pressing ⑥ or Ⓥ. To use the pull-down menus, select Very Large from the Font menu. Notice that the position number is highlighted in the status line.

Then select the Bold feature by pressing ⌷F6⌷ or selecting Appearance from the Font menu and then selecting Bold with the keyboard or mouse.

Now we're ready to type our header. Type "Trendy Togs, Incorporated" and press the ⌷→⌷ key twice to switch off the attributes codes that were set. Then press the ⌷Enter⌷ key twice and type the following:

```
"Trendy Styles Enter
for Little Smiles" Enter
```

Inserting figures   Now we'll add a graphic to our letterhead. First move the cursor to the "T" of "Trendy Togs". Activate the Graphics feature by pressing ⌷Alt⌷+⌷F9⌷, then select the Figure option by pressing ⌷1⌷ or ⌷F⌷ and select Options by pressing ⌷4⌷ or ⌷O⌷. To use the pull-down menus, select Figure from the Graphics menu and then select Options.

```
Options: Figure
    1 - Border Style
            Left                        Single
            Right                       Single
            Top                         Single
            Bottom                      Single
    2 - Outside Border Space
            Left                        0.167"
            Right                       0.167"
            Top                         0.167"
            Bottom                      0.167"
    3 - Inside Border Space
            Left                        0"
            Right                       0"
            Top                         0"
            Bottom                      0"
    4 - First Level Numbering Method    Numbers
    5 - Second Level Numbering Method   Off
    6 - Caption Number Style            [BOLD]Figure 1[bold]
    7 - Position of Caption             Below box, Outside borders
    8 - Minimum Offset from Paragraph   0"
    9 - Gray Shading (% of black)       0%
Selection: 0
```

The Options Figure submenu

In the submenu that appears, press ⌷1⌷ or ⌷B⌷ or click with the mouse to select the Border Style option. A menu appears at the bottom of the screen and the first setting in this option is highlighted. Since we do not want a border around our header, select the None setting by pressing ① or Ⓝ. The word "None" will now appear in the Border/Left option. Repeat this process until each option in Border Style is set to "None". When you're finished, press Exit (F7 or select Exit from the File menu) to return to the header.

Now activate the Graphics feature again by pressing Alt+F9 and select the Figure option by pressing ① or Ⓕ. Then select the Create option by pressing ① or Ⓒ. To use the pull-down menus, select Figure from the Graphics menu and then select Create with the keyboard or the mouse.

From the submenu that appears, select the Filename option by pressing ① or Ⓕ or clicking with the mouse. After the Enter filename: prompt, type BURST-1.WPG and then press Enter.

Next press ⑦ or Ⓢ or click with the mouse to activate the Size option. In the menu that appears in the status line, select the Set Height/Auto Width option by pressing ②.

```
Definition: Figure

    1 - Filename              BURST-1.WPG

    2 - Contents              Graphic

    3 - Caption

    4 - Anchor Type           Paragraph

    5 - Vertical Position     0"

    6 - Horizontal Position   Right

    7 - Size                  3.25" wide x 2.35" (high)

    8 - Wrap Text Around Box  Yes

    9 - Edit


Height = 3.25"
```

Setting the height

At the `Height:` prompt type "0.9"" and then press `Enter`. Press Exit (`F7`) until you return to the normal editing screen.

The header will not appear on the screen. But it is possible to see what it will look like when it is printed by using the View Document feature. To activate this feature, press `Shift`+`F7` and then press `6` or `V` or click with the mouse. To use the pull-down menus, select Print from File menu. Select the 100% option by pressing the `1` key. When you're finished, return to the Edit mode by pressing Exit (`F7`).

To save this document, activate Save by pressing `F10` or selecting Save from the File menu. At the `Document to be saved:` prompt, type HEADER and press `Enter`. You now have a header that can be used as a letterhead on various correspondence.

This completes our chapter on creating documents. You've learned a lot in this chapter and have practiced using what you've learned. Now that you have some basic knowledge about how WordPerfect operates, you can begin to create your own documents.

The following tables list the key combinations and menu options of commands discussed in this section.

Action	Key combination
Bold	`F6`
Double underline	`Ctrl`+`F8`,`2`,`3`
	`Ctrl`+`F8`,`A`,`D`
Graphic load	`Alt`+`F9`,`1`,`1`,`1`
	`Alt`+`F9`,`F`,`C`,`F`
Header	`Shift`+`F8`,`2`,`3`
	`Shift`+`F8`,`P`,`H`
Switch	`Shift`+`F3`
Underline	`F8`
Very large font	`Ctrl`+`F8`,`1`,`6`
	`Ctrl`+`F8`,`S`,`V`

Action	Menu selection
Bold	Font/Appearance/Bold
Double underline	Font/Appearance/Double Underline
Graphic load	Graphics/Figure/Create/Filename
Header	Layout/Page/Headers
Switch	Edit/Switch Document
Underline	Font/Appearance/Underline
Very large font	Font/Very Large

5. Using Macros

In this chapter we'll discuss one of WordPerfect's most powerful features—the Macro feature. As you'll see, you can save much time and energy by using macros. First we'll explain what macros are and then we'll present some examples so that you can learn how to use them in your documents.

Although you may have never heard of a macro before, don't be intimidated by them. After working through this chapter, you should feel more comfortable using them. By mastering macros, you'll be closer to using WordPerfect to its full potential.

What's a macro? Basically a macro is a collection of instructions that can be saved and used again at any time. In WordPerfect, a macro is a group of keystrokes that can either contain text or procedures (actions that should be performed).

For example, when you create letters, either personal or business, there are several elements that are always the same in each letter, such as your return address. Instead of having to type in your address each time you create a letter, you could use a macro, which would automatically insert your address into your letters for you. Another way to use a macro is to perform repetitive procedures automatically.

Suppose that you use the same page format for many of the letters you create. As we learned in Chapter 4, format adjustment requires selecting various options and settings. However, you could create a macro that would automatically make these settings for you. So you wouldn't have to repeat the same steps each time you create a certain type of letter.

To use macros in WordPerfect, we must use the Macro feature. This feature has two parts. First a macro must be created (defined), which involves recording the keystrokes you perform. Then a macro can be activated (executed), which performs the stored keystrokes.

Now that you know what macros are, let's try to create a sample macro of our own.

5.1 Defining a Macro

In this section we'll create a macro that will record the text for a return address and a macro that will make some formatting settings. First be sure that you're located in the normal editing screen. Then activate the Macro Define feature by pressing [Ctrl]+[F10] or by selecting Macro from the Tools menu and then selecting Define using the keyboard or mouse. You should see the following prompt in the status line on your screen:

```
Define macro:
```

Activating Macro Define

After this prompt, you must enter a name for your macro before you can create it. However, this is more involved than simply entering a macro name. There are three ways you can name a macro and each method has its own advantages and disadvantages.

One way to name a macro is to enter a macro name that contains up to eight characters. By using this method you can give the macro a name that describes the actions that are performed. This makes it easier to remember what a specific macro does, which is useful when you have a large number of macros. Another way to name a macro is to hold down the [Alt] key and press one of the letter keys (A-Z). This method enables you to execute a macro quickly because you don't have to activate the Macro feature when you want to execute this type of macro. You simply press the [Alt] key combination you specified and the macro executes automatically.

The third way to name a macro is by pressing the [Enter] key; you don't have to enter a macro name or a description. When you use this method, the default macro is created. WordPerfect automatically names this macro WP{WP}.WPM. Since this macro is the default macro, it will be executed automatically when you activate Macro and press the [Enter] key. You don't have to enter its macro name.

Regardless of which method you use to name your macros, WordPerfect will add the .WPM extension to them and then save them in the default directory. It's also possible to store your macros in other directories instead of the default directory. For more information on how to do this, consult your WordPerfect manual.

Let's use the [Enter] key method to name our macro. To do this, press the [Enter] key. The Macro Def message will begin to flash in the status line.

Note: If we were using one of the other methods for naming macros, first the Description: prompt would appear in the status line.

139

```
┌──────────────────────────────────────────────────────────────────────┐
│                                                                        │
│                                                                        │
│                                                                        │
│                                                                        │
│                                                                        │
│                                                                        │
│                                                                        │
│                                                                        │
│                                                                        │
│                                                                        │
│                                                                        │
│                                                                        │
│                                                                        │
│                                                                        │
│                                                                        │
│ Macro Def                                      Doc 1 Pg 1 Ln 1" Pos 1" │
└──────────────────────────────────────────────────────────────────────┘
```

Defining a macro

Once this message appears, WordPerfect will record all the keystrokes you make. So it's important to carefully plan what you want to do before actually pressing the keys. Now enter the following lines, exactly as they appear; press Enter after each line:

```
Brian Ward
1000 Cleaver Street
San Diego CA 93401
```

Note: Don't worry if you make a mistake while creating a macro. At any point during macro recording, you can activate Macro Define, by pressing Ctrl+F10 or selecting Macro from the Tools menu and then selecting Define, to stop the macro recording. Then restart the entire process from the beginning and use the same name or Alt key combination again.

If you're rewriting a macro that was named using the Alt key method or the macro name method, a message, indicating that the macro was already defined, will appear. Simply select the Replace option. If you used the [Enter] method with the macro you're rewriting this type of prompt will not appear. The default macro will automatically be replaced.

It's also possible to edit macros instead of rewriting them. We'll discuss editing macros later in this chapter.

When you're finished, activate Macro Define again by pressing [Ctrl]+[F10] or by selecting Macro from the Tools menu and then selecting Define. This will switch off the macro recording. Press Exit ([F7]) and then press [N] twice to clear the screen and remain in WordPerfect.

Now we'll create another macro but this time we'll use a different method for naming the macro. As we mentioned earlier, macros can also be used to record procedures as well as text. For example, if the same format is used for all your personal correspondence, you could create a macro that would automatically make these formatting settings so that you wouldn't have to enter them every time you wrote a letter.

Let's try doing this now. First activate the Macro Define feature by pressing [Ctrl]+[F10] or by selecting Macro from the Tools menu and then selecting Define. The `Define macro:` prompt will appear in the status line. This time we'll use the [Alt] key method for naming macros. Hold down the [Alt] key and press [F]. The `Description:` prompt should appear on your screen.

At this prompt you can enter a brief summary (up to 39 characters) of what the macro does. This can be helpful if you ever forget what actions a certain macro performs. However, entering a description for a macro is not required in order to create a macro. If you want to skip this prompt, simply press [Enter]. Let's enter a summary for our macro. Type the following:

```
Sets format for personal letters
```

When you're finished, press [Enter]. Now the `Macro Def` message will flash in the status line.

Note: Although the mouse can be used to access the pull-down menus while you're defining a macro, it cannot be used to move the cursor. Instead, you must use the arrow keys.

Now activate the Format Page submenu by pressing [Shift]+[F 8] and pressing [2] or [P] or by selecting Page from the Layout menu with the keyboard or the mouse. Select the Center Page (top to bottom) option by pressing [1] or [C] or clicking on it with the mouse. Then press [Y] to turn on this option.

Next, press Cancel [F1] to return to the Format submenu. Now select the Line option by pressing the [1] or [L] keys or clicking with the mouse. In the menu that appears, select the Justification option by pressing [3] or [J] or by clicking with the mouse and select the Left setting by pressing [1] or [L]. Then select the Margins - Left/Right option by pressing [7] or [M]. Type "2.5"", press [Enter], type "2.5"" and then press [Enter] again.

Press Exit ([F 7]) until you reach the normal editing screen. To switch off the macro recording, activate Macro Define again by pressing [Ctrl]+[F10] or by selecting Macro from the Tools menu and then selecting Define.

5.2 Executing a Macro

In this section we'll show you how to execute the macros you just created. How a macro is executed depends on the method that was used for naming the macro when it was defined. Before we execute our macros, we need a document into which the macro can be entered. First press Exit (F7) and then press N twice to clear the screen and remain in WordPerfect.

Before executing a macro, you must ensure that the cursor is located in the proper location. For example, since the macro we just created will affect the format of the document, the cursor must be located at the very beginning of the document.

Let's activate this macro first. Since we used the Alt key method to name this macro, it can by activated by simply pressing Alt+F. Do this now.

```
                                        Doc 1 Pg 1 Ln 1" Pos 2.5"
```

Screen after macro is activated

The `Please wait` message briefly flashed on the screen. Then, if you look at your screen closely, you'll see that the cursor has moved, which is indicated by the position number in the status line. Now let's see whether the macro made the appropriate settings for our document. To do this, activate the Reveal Codes feature by pressing [Alt]+[F3] or selecting Reveal Codes from the Edit menu using the keyboard or the mouse. The following should appear on your screen:

```
                ^         ^      ^    ^   ^   ^     ^   ^          Doc 1 Pg 1 Ln 1" Pos 2.5"
                         {                             }          ^     ^     ^      ^
[Center Pg][Just:Left][L/R Mar:2.5",2.5"]








Press Reveal Codes to restore screen
```

Displaying the settings made by the macro

As you can see, the macro inserted the proper codes into the document. Activate Reveal Codes again to return to the normal editing screen. Now let's activate the first macro we created. Since the macro will insert a return address, which is the first item in a letter, the cursor should be located at the beginning of the document.

The process for executing this macro will differ from the previous one because we used a different method of naming the macro. To execute this macro, activate the Macro feature by pressing [Alt]+[F10] or selecting Macro from the Tools menu and then selecting Execute.

```
┌─────────────────────────────────────────────────────────────────────┐
│                                                                       │
│                                                                       │
│                                                                       │
│                                                                       │
│                                                                       │
│                                                                       │
│                                                                       │
│                                                                       │
│                                                                       │
│                                                                       │
│                                                                       │
│                                                                       │
│                                                                       │
│                                                                       │
│                                                                       │
│                                                                       │
│                                                                       │
│                                                                       │
Macro:                                                                  │
└───────────────────────────────────────────────────────────────────── 
```

Executing a macro

Since we used [Enter] to name our macro, we can simply press [Enter] at this prompt. The macro will be executed automatically.

Note: If we had entered a macro name for this macro, we would enter the name after the Macro: prompt and then press the [Enter] key.

The following should appear on your screen:

```
┌─────────────────────────────────────────────────────────────────┐
│        Brian Ward                                                 │
│        1000 Cleaver Street                                        │
│        San Diego CA 93401                                         │
│                                                                   │
│                                                                   │
│                                                                   │
│                                                                   │
│                                                                   │
│                                                                   │
│                                                                   │
│                                                                   │
│                                                                   │
│                                                                   │
│                                                                   │
│                                       Doc 1 Pg 1 Ln 1.5" Pos 2.5" │
└─────────────────────────────────────────────────────────────────┘
```

Text is inserted by macro

As you can see, creating macros isn't as complicated as it may at first seem. Although the examples we used are simple, you should now have an understanding of what macros are and how to use them. In the next section we'll discuss how to change existing macros.

Editing macros

In addition to defining and executing macros, WordPerfect enables you to edit existing macros. This is especially useful when you have a complicated macro that contains many instructions, but you only need to make a few changes. By using the Macro Editor, you can make the necessary changes without having to recreate the entire macro.

In this section we'll edit the macro, which we created in the previous section, that inserts the return address in a letter. Suppose that the zip code in the address should be changed to "93411".

Before starting the editing process, clear your screen by pressing Exit ((F7) or selecting Exit from the File menu with the keyboard or mouse). Then activate Macro Define by pressing (Ctrl)+(F10) or selecting Macro from the Tools menu and then selecting Define with the keyboard or mouse.

The `Define macro:` prompt appears in the status line. Now we must enter the name or (Alt) key combination of the macro to be edited. In this case the macro was named with (Enter). Even though we can execute this macro without entering its name, in order to edit this macro we must enter its name at this prompt. If you don't enter its name and simply press (Enter), this macro will automatically be overwritten without a confirmation prompt. Type WP{WP} and press (Enter).

```
WP{WP}.WPM Already Exists: 1 Replace; 2 Edit; 3 Description: 0
```

Activating the Macro Editor

You are informed that the macro you entered already exists. In the menu that appears, you have the choice of either replacing the macro, editing the macro or entering a new description for the macro. Select the Edit option by pressing ② or Ⓔ. The Macro Editor appears and your macro is displayed:

```
┌────────────────────────────────────────────────────────────────────┐
│Macro: Action                                                         │
│                                                                      │
│    File              WP{WP}.WPM                                      │
│                                                                      │
│    Description                                                       │
│   ┌─────────────────────────────────────────────────────────────┐   │
│   │{DISPLAY OFF}Brian Ward{Enter}                                 │   │
│   │1000 Cleaver Street{Enter}                                     │   │
│   │San Diego CA 93401{Enter}                                      │   │
│   │                                                               │   │
│   │                                                               │   │
│   │                                                               │   │
│   │                                                               │   │
│   │                                                               │   │
│   │                                                               │   │
│   │                                                               │   │
│   │                                                               │   │
│   │                                                               │   │
│   │                                                               │   │
│   └─────────────────────────────────────────────────────────────┘   │
│Ctrl-PgUp for macro commands;   Press Exit when done                  │
└────────────────────────────────────────────────────────────────────┘
```

The Macro Editor screen

At the top of the screen the macro name and description, if available, are displayed. In this screen it's possible to insert and delete text and commands. The cursor can be moved in the same ways as when you're in the normal editing screen. If your macro is long and contains many instructions, you can also make formatting changes to the macro so that it is easier to read.

Now let's change the zip code to "93411". To do this, move the cursor to the "0" and press the (Del) key. Then type "1". The zip code has now been corrected. To leave the Macro Editor screen, press Exit by pressing (F7). (Do not use the pull-down menus to select Exit while in the Macro Editor screen.) You will be returned to the normal editing screen.

Let's execute this macro to see the changes we just made. To do this, activate Macro by pressing (Alt)+(F10) or by selecting Macro from the Tools menu and then selecting Execute. When the Macro: prompt appears, press (Enter).

```
Brian Ward
1000 Cleaver Street
San Diego CA 93411




















                                    Doc 1 Pg 1 Ln 1.5" Pos 1"
```

Displaying the edited macro

As you can see, the zip code has been changed accordingly. Also notice that the format settings we made with the (Alt)+(F) macro, from the previous section, weren't inserted. This happened because we only activated the macro containing the return address and not the macro containing the formatting settings.

Adding a pause So far the macros we've created have executed without stopping during their execution. This is suitable when macros don't need any additional information in order to complete their tasks. However, sometimes you may need to enter data at some point during the macro execution. WordPerfect enables you to pause macro execution so that you can enter text from the keyboard and then continue the macro execution.

Let's add a pause to the macro we just edited. Suppose that you want to use the same greeting and first line in your letters. We can edit the macro so it will do this. However, since the greeting would be used in letters to different people, the macro should pause so that you can

149

enter the appropriate name after the greeting. Then it should continue to enter the first line of the letter.

First clear the screen by pressing Exit ((F7) or select Exit from the File menu) and pressing (N) twice. Now activate Macro Define by pressing (Ctrl)+(F10) or by selecting Macro from the Tools menu and then selecting Define. Type "wp{wp}" and press (Enter). Select the Edit option by pressing (2) or (E); the Macro Editor screen appears again.

Now we'll insert some blank lines before entering our greeting. First move the cursor to the blank line after the last line of the macro. To insert a blank line, you must press the (Enter) key. However, in order to insert (Enter), Exit and Cancel in a macro while in the Macro Editor screen, you must press (Ctrl)+(V) first. If you don't do this, WordPerfect will perform the required function instead of inserting the instruction in the macro. Press (Ctrl)+(V) and then press (Enter). Repeat this process until six {Enter} instructions are inserted. Then enter the greeting "Dear(Spacebar)".

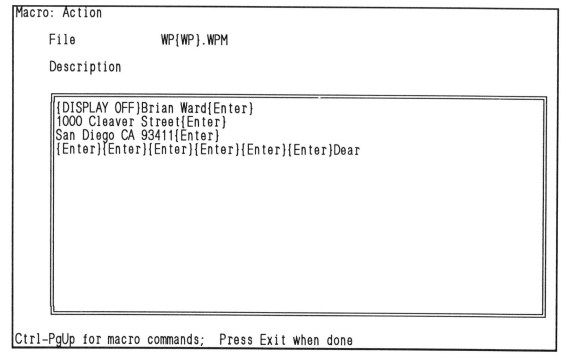

```
Macro: Action

    File              WP{WP}.WPM

    Description

  ┌─────────────────────────────────────────────────────────────┐
  │{DISPLAY OFF}Brian Ward{Enter}                                 │
  │1000 Cleaver Street{Enter}                                     │
  │San Diego CA 93411{Enter}                                      │
  │{Enter}{Enter}{Enter}{Enter}{Enter}{Enter}Dear                 │
  │                                                               │
  │                                                               │
  │                                                               │
  │                                                               │
  │                                                               │
  │                                                               │
  │                                                               │
  │                                                               │
  └─────────────────────────────────────────────────────────────┘

Ctrl-PgUp for macro commands;   Press Exit when done
```

Entering changes

The cursor is now located where the pause should appear.

Notice the menu at the bottom of the screen. In order to insert a pause, we must use the macro programming language commands (we'll discuss the macro language later in this chapter). To display a list of these commands, press Ctrl + Pg Up.

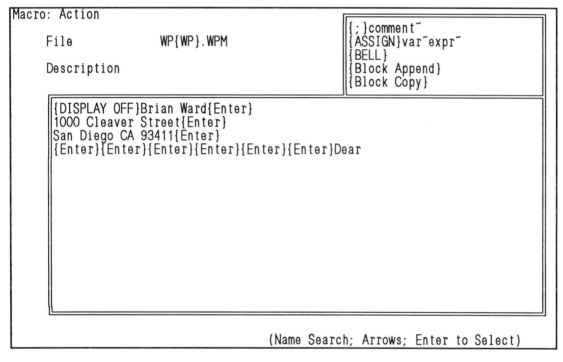

Activating the macro language commands

The macro language commands appear in their own box in the upper-right portion of the screen. Press the ↓ key until {PAUSE} is selected. Then press Enter; you'll see that a pause is inserted in the macro.

Now let's enter the first line of the letter. To do this, press Ctrl + V and then Enter. Repeat this process again so that two Enter instructions are inserted. Then type the following:

```
How are you? I thought I would write to tell you about my great news.
```

To return to the normal editing screen, press Exit (F7). Now let's execute both of our macros. First press Alt+F to execute the first macro. Then activate Macro by pressing Alt+F10 or by selecting Macro from the Tools menu and then selecting Execute. When the Macro: prompt appears, press Enter. The macro will execute and then pause so that you can enter the recipient's name.

```
Brian Ward
1000 Cleaver Street
San Diego CA 93411




Dear









                                              Doc 1 Pg 1 Ln 2.5" Pos 3"
```

The macro pauses

Type "Bob," and then press Enter. Then the macro execution continues. Your screen should look similar to the following:

```
┌─────────────────────────────────────────────────────────┐
│    Brian Ward                                             │
│    1000 Cleaver Street                                    │
│    San Diego CA 93411                                     │
│                                                           │
│                                                           │
│                                                           │
│                                                           │
│    Dear Bob,                                              │
│                                                           │
│    How are you? I thought I would                         │
│    write to tell you about my great                       │
│    news.                                                  │
│                                                           │
│                                                           │
│                                                           │
│                                                           │
│                                                           │
│                                                           │
│                                                           │
│                          Doc 1 Pg 1 Ln 3.17" Pos 3"       │
└─────────────────────────────────────────────────────────┘
```

The macro execution is complete

As you can see, the macro execution is completed. Now the remaining text of the letter can be entered.

Congratulations, you've now successfully created, executed and edited macros. Since you now have some basic knowledge about macros, you can begin to save time and work more efficiently by creating your own macros.

Advanced macro features

Since this is a beginner's book, we've only covered the basics of using macros in WordPerfect. Consequently, the macros we created in the previous sections perform very simple operations. However, the WordPerfect Macro feature is also capable of performing very complex operations. We'll provide a brief overview of some of these features in this section. For more information and instructions, refer to your WordPerfect manual.

5.3 Chaining and Nesting Macros

With WordPerfect it's possible to combine macros so that by activating one, another macro or several macros will automatically be executed. So you don't have to activate each macro separately.

One way to do this is to *chain* macros. This means that when one macro ends, another will automatically begin. When you use this procedure, the macro you activated either starts itself again or starts a different macro when it is finished executing.

Nesting macros is similar to chaining macros except that when macros are nested, they are placed within each other. So instead of waiting for the first macro to complete, the nested macro is executed while the first macro is still being executed. Basically the operation of the first macro is interrupted so that the nested macro can run. Once the nested macro is completed, the first macro will continue to run.

Macro programming language

WordPerfect's macro feature also contains a macro programming language, which can be used to create very complex macros. By using this language, you can create macros that contain logical structures, such as if/then, and variables, for example.

To use the macro programming language, you must use the Macro Editor, which we discussed in the previous section. Using the Macro Editor to create and edit macros differs from creating macros from the keyboard. Instead of performing actions, which are then recorded, you insert text, keystrokes and macro programming commands in the Macro Editor screen.

The following tables list the key combinations and menu options of commands discussed in this section.

Action	Key combination
Center page	[Shift]+[F 8],[2],[1]
	[Shift]+[F 8],[P],[C]
Define macro	[Ctrl]+[F10]
Execute macro	[Alt]+[F10]
Left justification	[Shift]+[F 8],[1],[3],[1]
	[Shift]+[F 8],[L],[J],[L]
Left/right margins	[Shift]+[F 8],[1],[7]
	[Shift]+[F 8],[L],[M]

Action	Menu selection
Center page	Layout/Page/Center Page
Define macro	Tools/Macro/Define
Execute macro	Tools/Macro/Execute
Left justification	Layout/Justify/Left
Left/right margins	Layout/Line/Margins

6. Merging Documents

In this chapter we'll present the WordPerfect feature Merge. With this feature, which is also called *mail-merge* because it is mainly used to create form letters and mailing labels, you can combine information from two or more sources into one document. This feature is extremely helpful when you must send the same letter, or other type of document (e.g., a memo), to many different people or when only certain parts of a document should be changed. So, these documents are identical except for certain pieces of information.

Note: Although Merge can be used with a variety of documents, to simplify our discussion, we'll refer to the document that will be created with Merge as a "letter".

Obviously, using this feature can save you much time when you need to create many letters. For example, if you needed to send the same letter to 100 people, by using Merge you would only have to create two documents, instead of 100, to accomplish this task.

Before demonstrating how to use Merge, you must understand the different elements that are needed in order for a merge process to work.

Merge elements   The Merge feature requires two *sources* in order to operate. These sources contain the information that will be used to create the merged document.

One kind of source is the *primary file*, which is required for the merge process. This document contains the information that will be the same for each copy of the letter. Basically the primary file is the same as a normal WordPerfect document except that it contains merge commands. These commands control the merge process by indicating where in the document data should be inserted.

The primary file looks to other sources for specific information. One source is the *secondary file*, which contains the information that will be inserted into the primary file. Secondary files are also called *address files*. These files contain the information that will change in each copy of the letter. This information is inserted at the appropriate location in the primary file.

Secondary files are further divided into *records*, which contain a group of related information. The information from one record will be inserted into one copy of the letter. Each record is separated by a END RECORD merge command (we'll discuss merge commands later in this chapter) and a Hard Page break, which appears on the screen as a double line of dashes. Records can contain an unlimited amount of information, and the amount of disk space you have available determines how many records you can have in your secondary file.

The information in each record is divided into *fields*. One field contains one of the items that will be inserted into the primary file. At the end of each field an END FIELD merge code and then a hard return is inserted. Although it's possible to have an unlimited amount of fields in a record, each record in the secondary file must contain the same number of fields. Also, the fields in one of the records should contain the same type of information as the fields in the other records. For example, if the records contain mailing addresses, the fields of each record will contain different portions of the mailing address.

Here's a summary of these terms:

RECORD   This is the "page" of data. Think of a box of file cards containing addresses. Each file card is the paper equivalent of a record, as it contains all the data needed for one person's address.

FIELD   Each file card contains individual lines of data (the person's name, address, phone number, etc.). These lines of data represent fields as described in this chapter.

Other sources that can be used with the primary file are the keyboard, document files and the Shell Clipboard. Instead of a secondary file, you can use the keyboard to enter the information that will change with each copy of the letter. When the appropriate information is needed, the Merge process stops so that you can enter the information from the keyboard. This is useful if you only have a small number of letters to create. Another source that can be used is document files, which contain sections of text that can be inserted into the primary file at specific locations. This process is also called "document assembly". If you have the WordPerfect Shell, the Shell Clipboard can be used as a primary or secondary file. Refer to your WordPerfect manual for more information about any of these sources.

6.1 Creating Sources

In this section we'll create a primary file and a secondary file that we'll merge. First we'll create our secondary file so that we can establish which fields we'll use. The document we want to create is a letter informing customers that a product they've ordered has arrived. Since there are four customers, we'll need four records in our secondary file. In each record we'll use four fields: one for the customer's name, one for their mailing address, one for the salutation and one for the product name.

The secondary file Before creating the secondary document, clear the screen by pressing Exit (F7 or select Exit from the File menu).

Fields can be referenced by either numbers or names. Since it's easier to remember the contents of a field if it has a name instead of a number, we'll use names in our example.

Note: If you want to use field numbers instead of names, simply type the information for the first field and then activate the END FIELD command by pressing F9 or by selecting Merge Codes from the Tools menu, selecting More and then selecting END FIELD from the merge commands box.

In order to do this we must insert the FIELD NAMES merge command first. To do this, activate the Merge Codes feature by pressing Shift+F9 and selecting the More option by pressing 6 or M or by pressing Shift+F9 twice. To use the pull-down menus, select Merge Codes from the Tools menu and then select More by using the keyboard or the mouse. The following should appear on your screen:

```
[{ASSIGN}var~expr~                                        ]
|{BELL}
|{BREAK}
|{CALL}label~
|{CANCEL OFF}
|{CANCEL ON}
|{CASE}expr~cs1~lb1~...csN~lbN~~
|{CASE CALL}expr~cs1~lb1~...csN~lbN~~
|{CHAIN MACRO}macroname~                          (^G)
|{CHAIN PRIMARY}filename~
```

(Name Search; Arrows; Enter to Select)

Activating Merge Codes

The box that appears in the upper-right corner of your screen contains the list of merge commands. To select the FIELD NAMES command, either use the arrow keys to highlight it or start typing its name until it is highlighted in the list. Press the [Enter] key once this command is highlighted.

```
{DOCUMENT}filename~
{ELSE}
{END FIELD}                           (^R)
{END FOR}
{END IF}
{END RECORD}                          (^E)
{END WHILE}
{FIELD}field~                         (^F)
[{FIELD NAMES}name1~...nameN~~        ]
{FOR}var~start~stop~step~
```

Enter Field 1:

Activating the FIELD NAMES command

Now we'll enter the names for our fields. After the Enter Field 1: prompt, type "Name" and press (Enter). The prompt will now change to Enter Field 2:; type "Address" and press (Enter). Then type "Salutation" and press (Enter); then type "Product" and press (Enter).

Note: Do not insert Hard Returns (by pressing the (Enter) key) after the fields or records of a secondary file. Doing this may interfere with the spacing in the merged document.

To switch off this command, activate Merge Codes again by pressing (Shift)+(F9). (You cannot use the pull-down menus to do this.) You should see the following on your screen:

161

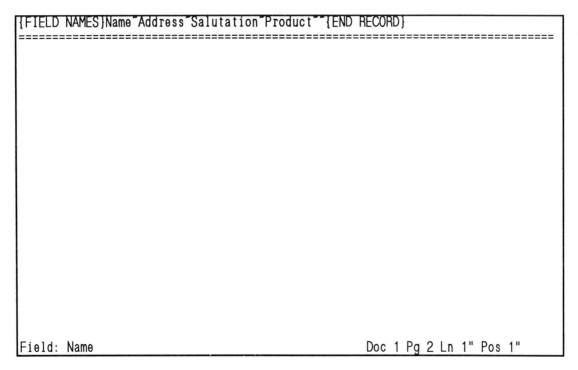

```
{FIELD NAMES}Name~Address~Salutation~Product~~{END RECORD}
============================================================================





















Field: Name                                    Doc 1 Pg 2 Ln 1" Pos 1"
```

Entering field names

As you can see, an END RECORD command and a Hard Page break were automatically inserted. The field names appear at the top of the screen and the cursor appears below the names. The message at the bottom of the screen indicates the name or number of the field where the cursor is currently located.

It's possible to place the field names on separate lines so that they are easier to read. To do this, move the cursor to the "N" of "Name" and press Enter. Now move the cursor to the beginning of the next field name and press Enter. Repeat this for each field name until each one is located on a separate line. When you reach the END RECORD command, move the cursor to the tilde character before the command and then press Enter.

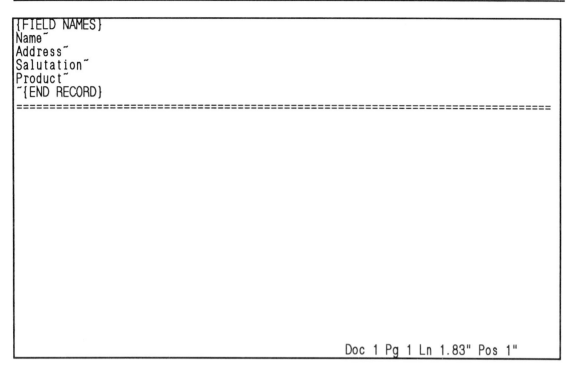

```
{FIELD NAMES}
Name~
Address~
Salutation~
Product~
~{END RECORD}
========================================================================
```
Doc 1 Pg 1 Ln 1.83" Pos 1"

Moving the field names

Each command and field name is located on its own line. Press the ⬇ key to return the cursor to its original location. The message at the bottom of the screen should read `Field: Name`. This indicates that the cursor is located at the Name field.

Now we can enter the fields for our first record. Let's enter the information for our first field. Type the following:

`Susan Baker`

Then press `F9` to insert the END FIELD code, or select Merge Codes from the Tools menu, select More and then select the END FIELD command from the list.

163

```
{FIELD NAMES}
Name~
Address~
Salutation~
Product~
~{END RECORD}
===============================================================================
Susan Baker{END FIELD}




















Field: Address                                        Doc 1 Pg 2 Ln 1.17" Pos 1"
```

Inserting the END FIELD command

The END FIELD command and a hard return code are automatically inserted after the name. Also notice that the cursor is now located at the Address field. Type the following information for the Address field and insert the END FIELD command (press [F9], or select Tools/Merge Codes/More/END FIELD):

```
50 Riverfront Road [Enter]
Grand Rapids MI 49511
```

Note: Although the Address field contains two lines, you can press [Enter] as you normally would to separate the lines. However, don't activate the END FIELD command until the end of the field (after the zip code).

Your screen should look similar to the following:

164

```
{FIELD NAMES}
Name˜
Address˜
Salutation˜
Product˜
˜{END RECORD}
===============================================================================
Susan Baker{END FIELD}
50 Riverfront Road
Grand Rapids MI 49511{END FIELD}




















Field: Salutation                              Doc 1 Pg 2 Ln 1.5" Pos 1"
```

Entering the Address field

Now enter the following information for the Salutation and Product fields (remember to insert an END FIELD command after each field—press (F9), or select Tools/Merge/Codes/More/END FIELD):

```
Ms. Baker:
legal pads
```

Once all the fields are entered, we must insert an END RECORD command. To do this, activate the Merge Codes feature by pressing (Shift)+(F9) and then select End Record by pressing (2) or (E) or select Merge Codes from the Tools menu and then select End Record. When you're finished, your screen should look similar to the following:

```
{FIELD NAMES}
Name~
Address~
Salutation~
Product~
~{END RECORD}
===============================================================================
Susan Baker{END FIELD}
50 Riverfront Road
Grand Rapids MI 49511{END FIELD}
Ms. Baker:{END FIELD}
legal pads{END FIELD}
{END RECORD}
===============================================================================




Field: Name                                           Doc 1 Pg 3 Ln 1" Pos 1"
```

Inserting an END RECORD command

The first record of our secondary file is now complete. Notice that the END RECORD command automatically inserts a hard page break to separate the records.

Now we need to create three more records for our secondary file. Repeat the procedures we used for the first record and enter the following information for each field of the remaining records (the words in **BOLD TYPE** indicate when you should select END FIELD or END RECORD [press (Shift)+(F9),(2), or select Tools/Merge Codes/End Record]):

```
Harry Lawson END FIELD
371 Union (Enter)
Wyoming MI 48320 END FIELD
Mr. Lawson: END FIELD
staples END FIELD
END RECORD
Bertha Reynolds END FIELD
119 60th Street (Enter)
Kentwood MI 49500 END FIELD
```

```
Ms. Reynolds: END FIELD
envelopes END FIELD
END RECORD
Cindy Davis END FIELD
248 Pleasantview [Enter]
Grand Rapids MI 48142 END FIELD
Ms. Davis: END FIELD
batteries END FIELD
END RECORD
```

When you're finished your screen should look similar to the following:

```
{END RECORD}
================================================================
Harry Lawson{END FIELD}
371 Union
Wyoming MI 48320{END FIELD}
Mr. Lawson:{END FIELD}
staples{END FIELD}
{END RECORD}
================================================================
Bertha Reynolds{END FIELD}
119 60th Street
Kentwood MI 49500{END FIELD}
Ms. Reynolds:{END FIELD}
envelopes{END FIELD}
{END RECORD}
================================================================
Cindy Davis{END FIELD}
248 Pleasantview
Grand Rapids MI 48142{END FIELD}
Ms. Davis:{END FIELD}
batteries{END FIELD}
{END RECORD}
================================================================
Field: Name                          Doc 1 Pg 6 Ln 1" Pos 1"
```

All records entered

Once all the records are entered, the secondary file is complete. The next step is to save the file. Do this now by activating Save either by pressing [F10] or by selecting Save from the File menu with the keyboard or the mouse. Type "Info" and press [Enter]. Then clear the screen by pressing Exit ([F7] or selecting Exit from the File menu) and then the [N] key twice. Now we're ready to create our primary file.

The primary file   As we previously mentioned, the primary file contains the information that is the same for each copy of the letter. For our example primary file, we'll create a short letter that informs customers that the items they ordered have arrived. The names, addresses and products will be the information that will change with each letter. When we need to insert this information in the letter, we'll use the FIELD command at the appropriate location.

Before typing the text of our letter, first let's select some format settings. First we'll change the margin settings. To do this, activate the Format feature by pressing (Shift)+(F8) and select the Line option by pressing (L) or (1) or clicking with the mouse. To use the pull-down menus, select Line from the Layout menu with the keyboard or mouse. Now activate the Margins Left/Right option by pressing (7) or (M) or clicking with the mouse and type "2"" for both settings. Then press Cancel ((F1)) to return to the Format menu and activate the Page option by pressing (2) or (P) or clicking with the mouse. Select the Center Page (top to bottom) option by pressing (1) or (C) and clicking with the mouse. To turn on this option, press (Y). When you're finished, press Cancel ((F1)) until you reach the normal editing screen.

Now we're ready to enter the text of the letter. Type the following exactly as it appears:

```
River City Office Supply (Enter)
224 West Main (Enter)
Grand Rapids MI 49511 (Enter)
(Enter)
(Enter)
June 15, 1991 (Enter)
(Enter)
(Enter)
```

At this point, we must enter the information from one of the fields. To do this, activate the Merge Codes feature by pressing (Shift)+(F9) and then select Field by pressing (1) or (F) or by selecting Merge Codes from the Tools menu and then selecting Field using the keyboard or mouse.

The `Enter field:` prompt appears at the bottom of the screen. At this prompt you must insert the number or name of the prompt you want to insert. Since we are using field names, we must enter the appropriate name. The first field that must be inserted in the letter contains the names of the customers. So type "Name" and press (Enter). You should see the following on your screen:

```
River City Office Supply
224 West Main
Grand Rapids MI 49511


June 15, 1991


{FIELD}Name~




                                    Doc 1 Pg 1 Ln 2.33" Pos 1.5"
```

Inserting the Name and Address fields

This command will insert the appropriate customer name into our letter during the merge process. Now press (Enter) and activate the FIELD command again. Type "Address" after the Enter field: prompt and press (Enter). This command will insert the appropriate customer address into the letter.

Now press (Enter) twice and activate the Field command. The information from the salutation field should be inserted in this location. So type "Salutation" and press (Enter). The following should appear on your screen:

169

```
┌────────────────────────────────────────────────────────────────────┐
│River City Office Supply                                              │
│224 West Main                                                         │
│Grand Rapids MI 49511                                                 │
│                                                                      │
│                                                                      │
│June 15, 1991                                                         │
│                                                                      │
│                                                                      │
│{FIELD}Name˜                                                          │
│{FIELD}Address˜                                                       │
│                                                                      │
│                                                                      │
│{FIELD}Salutation˜                                                    │
│                                                                      │
│                                                                      │
│                                                                      │
│                                                                      │
│                                                                      │
│                                                                      │
│                                                                      │
│                                                                      │
│                                                                      │
│                                                                      │
│                              Doc 1 Pg 1 Ln 3" Pos 2.1"               │
└────────────────────────────────────────────────────────────────────┘
```

Inserting the Salutation field

Note:
Although we've used all the fields from our secondary file in our primary file, not all the fields entered in the secondary file have to be used in the primary file. Also, the fields can be entered in any order and can be used more than once in the primary file.

We're almost finished inserting the fields that will be used in the merged document. Now press the (Enter) key twice and type the following text exactly as it appears:

```
We're happy to inform you that the(Spacebar)
```

At this point, we must enter our last field, which contains the item that the customer ordered. To insert this field, activate the FIELD command and type "Product".

170

```
River City Office Supply
224 West Main
Grand Rapids MI 49511


June 15, 1991


{FIELD}Name~
{FIELD}Address~


{FIELD}Salutation~

We're happy to inform you that the {FIELD}Product~




                                         Doc 1 Pg 1 Ln 3.33" Pos 5.3"
```

Inserting the Product field

Now press the [Spacebar] once and type the remaining text of the letter:

```
you ordered have arrived. We are sorry for the delay and hope it didn't cause you
any inconvenience. If we can help you with anything else, please don't hesitate
to call or stop by. Thank you for your order and continued patronage.
```

Note: The text on your screen will appear differently than the lines above. Simply type the above text without pressing the [Enter] key.

Once the entire paragraph is entered, press the [Enter] key twice. Then type the following:

```
Becky MacGregor [Enter]
Manager [Enter]
```

Our primary file is now complete. Let's save this file by activating Save by pressing [F10], or by selecting Save from the File menu. Type

171

CUSTOMER and press (Enter). Your screen should look similar to the following:

```
River City Office Supply
224 West Main
Grand Rapids MI 49511


June 15, 1991


{FIELD}Name~
{FIELD}Address~


{FIELD}Salutation~

We're happy to inform you that the {FIELD}Product~ you ordered have
arrived. We are sorry for the delay and hope it didn't cause you
any inconvenience. If we can help you with anything else, please
don't hesitate to call or stop by. Thank you for your order and
continued patronage.

Becky MacGregor
Manager

C:\CUSTOMER                                      Doc 1 Pg 1 Ln 4.5" Pos 1.7"
```

Completed primary file

Now that both the primary and secondary files are created, we can merge the two of them to create four copies of the same document.

6.2 Combining Sources

In this section we'll show you how to merge the documents we just created. Before doing this, clear the screen by pressing [F7] or selecting Exit from the File menu and pressing [N] twice.

To start the merge process, activate Merge/Sort by pressing [Ctrl]+[F9] and then select the Merge option by pressing [1] or [M]. To use the pull-down menus, select Merge from the Tools menu.

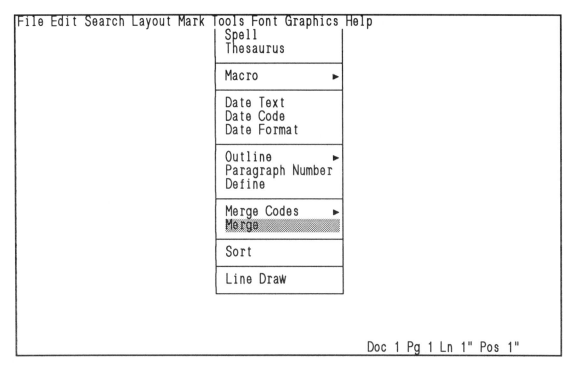

Activating the Merge option

After the Primary file: prompt, type "Customer" and press [Enter]. The Secondary file: prompt appears. Now type "Info" and press [Enter]. The merge process begins, which is indicated by the message "Merging", which flashes on your screen.

Note: To cancel the merge process, press Cancel ([F1]).

When the process is completed, you should see the following on your screen:

```
River City Office Supply
224 West Main
Grand Rapids MI 49511


June 15, 1991


Cindy Davis
248 Pleasantview
Grand Rapids MI 48142


Ms. Davis:

We're happy to inform you that the batteries you ordered have
arrived. We are sorry for the delay and hope it didn't cause you
any inconvenience. If we can help you with anything else, please
don't hesitate to call or stop by. Thank you for your order and
continued patronage.

Becky MacGregor
Manager
                                      Doc 1 Pg 4 Ln 4.67" Pos 1.7"
```

Merged document

The letter that appears contains the information from the last record of the secondary file. In our example, this is the letter addressed to the customer named "Cindy Davis". However, if you scroll the display up, you'll see that a letter, containing the information from each record, was created. The information from the fields were inserted in the appropriate locations in the letters. After each letter, WordPerfect automatically inserts a Hard Page code. This places the letters on separate pages.

You can now save and/or print the merged document. Saving the merged document isn't really necessary because the primary and secondary files are already saved. So, when you need the merged document you can always merge these two files again. Another reason why you may not want to save the merged document is if it is extremely large. If this is the case, it will take up too much space on your hard drive or on your floppy diskette.

This completes our chapter on merging documents. We've showed you the basics of using the Merge feature so that you can begin to use it to create your own merged documents. However, since this feature can be very complicated, you should refer to your WordPerfect manual for detailed information on special situations and for complete references to all of the merge commands.

Here's a summary of the keys and menu selections used in this chapter:

Action	Key combination	Menu selection
Merge codes	Shift + F9	Tools/Merge Codes
END FIELD	F9	Tools/Merge Codes/More/END FIELD
END RECORD	Shift + F9, 2	Tools/Merge Codes/End Record
FIELD	Shift + F9, 1	Tools/Merge Codes/Field
Merge/Sort	Ctrl + F9, 1	Tools/Merge

7. Printing Documents

After you've created documents using WordPerfect, you'll want to print them. WordPerfect provides various options for printing your documents. Although some of these options are more advanced than others, most of them are easy to use and understand.

In this chapter we'll discuss the different ways you can print documents with WordPerfect and introduce you to the basic options you'll need to know in order to print with WordPerfect. Since this is a beginners book, we won't discuss the more advanced printing features. So once you've read this chapter you should be able to print any of the documents you've created using the examples in this book.

Note: Before reading this chapter and performing the examples, we ask you to remember the following:

1) Be sure that your printer is selected. This is usually done when WordPerfect is installed. For more information, refer to your WordPerfect manual.

2) **IMPORTANT:** No two printers are alike. What printed out for us may not print for you, depending on the printer brand and type (dot matrix, laser, etc.). Before attempting any "serious" printing using WordPerfect, we recommend that you spend time getting acquainted with your printer if you haven't already done so. Experiment in WordPerfect with your printer. Enter a document consisting of the alphabet and print that, formatting the alphabet with different fonts and character styles to see what's available.

For more information about your printer, see your printer manual. For general information about printers, see the books *Tips & Tricks for your PC Printer* and *Laser Printer PowerTools*, both published by Abacus.

7.1 The Print Feature

One of the ways you can print a document in WordPerfect is by using the Print feature. By using Print, it's possible to print text from a variety of sources. You can print the entire document that is currently on your screen or that is located on disk (saved on your hard drive or a floppy diskette), specific pages of the document on screen or on disk, the document summary or a block of text that you've selected.

Let's activate this feature now by pressing [Shift]+[F7] or by selecting Print from the File menu with the keyboard or mouse.

```
Print

    1 - Full Document
    2 - Page
    3 - Document on Disk
    4 - Control Printer
    5 - Multiple Pages
    6 - View Document
    7 - Initialize Printer


Options

    S - Select Printer                    Standard Printer
    B - Binding Offset                    0"
    N - Number of Copies                  1
    U - Multiple Copies Generated by      WordPerfect
    G - Graphics Quality                  Medium
    T - Text Quality                      High




Selection: 0
```

The Print menu

The Print menu appears on the screen. The menu's options are divided into two sections. The options listed under Print at the top of the screen will affect the actual printing process and the options listed under Options at the bottom will affect how the printed documents will look.

As we mentioned, you have several options for printing text. To print the entire document that is currently located in the normal editing screen, you would select the Full Document option. Use the Page option when you want to print only the page on which the cursor is currently located. If you want to print selected pages of the document currently in the normal editing screen, use the Multiple Pages option.

With WordPerfect it's also possible to print a document that is saved on disk (on hard drive or floppy diskette). This is helpful because you don't have to retrieve the document to the normal editing screen in order to print it. To print a document that is on disk, you would use the Document on Disk option under `Print` in the Print menu. As with a document that is currently on the screen, you can also print selected pages of a document on disk.

Let's try using both of these methods now. First let's print a document that was saved on disk. We'll use the balance sheet we created in Chapter 4.

Note: If you saved the sample documents on your hard drive, as we did in our examples, you don't need to insert a floppy diskette. However, if you don't have a hard drive you'll need to insert the diskette containing your sample documents into drive A:.

Before performing the steps listed below be sure that your printer is properly connected to the computer. Also be sure that there is paper in the printer and that the printer is switched on and is online. Once you've done this, you should be ready to print.

To print a document that is on disk, activate the Document on Disk option by pressing ③ or Ⓓ or by clicking on the option with the mouse.

```
┌─────────────────────────────────────────────────────────────────────┐
│Print                                                                  │
│                                                                       │
│      1 - Full Document                                                │
│      2 - Page                                                         │
│      3 - Document on Disk                                             │
│      4 - Control Printer                                              │
│      5 - Multiple Pages                                              │
│      6 - View Document                                                │
│      7 - Initialize Printer                                          │
│                                                                       │
│                                                                       │
│Options                                                                │
│                                                                       │
│      S - Select Printer              Standard Printer                 │
│      B - Binding Offset              0"                               │
│      N - Number of Copies            1                                │
│      U - Multiple Copies Generated by  WordPerfect                    │
│      G - Graphics Quality            Medium                           │
│      T - Text Quality                High                             │
│                                                                       │
│                                                                       │
│                                                                       │
│                                                                       │
│Selection: 0                                                           │
└─────────────────────────────────────────────────────────────────────┘
```

Activating Document on Disk

The prompt `Document name:` appears in the status line. Type the filename "Balance" and press `Enter`. The `Page(s): (all)` message appears on the screen. If this sample document contained several pages and we wanted to print only one page or only a few selected pages, we would enter the appropriate pages after this message.

Since our document is only one page, we'll print the entire document. To do this, simply press `Enter`. The `* Please wait *` message briefly flashes in the status line and then the printer will begin to print the document.

Note:　　WordPerfect may display a message indicating that the document isn't formatted for the current printer. You can still print the document on the printer by pressing `Y`, but the formatting may not look the way you intended it to look on the printed copy.

Your sample balance sheet document should now be printed. If your printer still hasn't started, there are several possible causes. The printer may not be connected properly or it may not be online. Check your printer again and make any adjustments. If the printer still won't work, refer to your printer manual for instructions.

Now let's try to print a document that is located in the normal editing screen. This time we'll use our sample document QUARTER. First return to the normal editing screen by activating Exit (press F7 or select Exit from the File menu with the keyboard or mouse).

To retrieve the document, activate Retrieve (press Shift+F10 or select Retrieve from the File menu with the keyboard or mouse). After the Document to be retrieved: prompt type "Quarter" and then press Enter.

The document should appear on the screen. Now activate the Print feature (press Shift+F7 or select Print from the File menu with the keyboard or mouse). Then select the Full Document option by pressing 1 or F.

The * Please wait * message briefly flashes on the screen and the printer begins to print the document.

Printing a block of text

WordPerfect also allows you to print a block of text from a document that is currently in the normal editing screen. This is helpful when you want to print only a certain passage from a document instead of the entire document.

Let's try to print a block of text from our sample document QUARTER. First return to the normal editing screen by pressing Cancel (F1) or Exit (F7 or select Exit from the File menu).

Suppose that you want to print only the second paragraph of this letter. To do this, we must first select this paragraph by using the Block feature. Move the cursor to the "P" of "Profit" and activate Block by pressing Alt+F4 or by selecting Block from the Edit menu.

The Block on message will begin to flash in the status line. Now select the text, using the arrow keys or the mouse, until the entire paragraph is selected. Your screen should look similar to the following:

181

```
┌──────────────────────────────────────────────────────────┐
│         TO OUR SHAREHOLDERS                                │
│                                                            │
│         Current market conditions indicate that Trendy     │
│         Togs, Inc. will continue to build upon the         │
│         gains displayed in this 1991 second quarter        │
│         report.                                            │
│                                                            │
│            [Profit climed 20% over first                   │
│            quarter. Sales are up 30%.                      │
│            Stockholders' equity jumped by                  │
│            $400,000. The best news is the                  │
│            company's ratio of current assets to            │
│            current liabilities. It is now 3.0,             │
│            a full 1.0 higher than this time last year.]    │
│                                                            │
│         The company recently purchased Baby Bottoms, a     │
│         local designer diaper manufacturer. Baby           │
│         Bottles has been relatively stagnant over the      │
│         last five years, but we fully intend to            │
│         increase volume through Trendy Togs' strong        │
│         sales and distribution network within the next     │
│         year. This support, combined with Trendy Togs'     │
│         new line of designer baby clothes, should          │
│ Block on                              Doc 1 Pg 1 Ln 3.5" Pos 3.5" │
└──────────────────────────────────────────────────────────┘
```

Paragraph is selected

Now activate Print by pressing [Shift]+[F7] or by selecting Print from the File menu. The `Print Block? No (Yes)` prompt appears.

```
TO OUR SHAREHOLDERS

Current market conditions indicate that Trendy
Togs, Inc. will continue to build upon the
gains displayed in this 1991 second quarter
report.

     [Profit climed 20% over first
      quarter. Sales are up 30%.
      Stockholders' equity jumped by
      $400,000. The best news is the
      company's ratio of current assets to
      current liabilities. It is now 3.0,
      a full 1.0 higher than this time last year.]

The company recently purchased Baby Bottoms, a
local designer diaper manufacturer. Baby
Bottles has been relatively stagnant over the
last five years, but we fully intend to
increase volume through Trendy Togs' strong
sales and distribution network within the next
year. This support, combined with Trendy Togs'
new line of designer baby clothes, should
Print block? No (Yes)
```

Printing a block of text

Press Ⓨ to answer the `Print block? No (Yes)` message that appears in the status line. Once you do this, the `* Please wait *` message will flash briefly and the block of text will be printed.

Notice that the same page format that was used to print the entire document was used to print the block. For example, the paragraph is centered between the top and bottom margins of the page just as the entire document was centered between the top and bottom margins.

As we mentioned, it's also possible to print the document summary for a document on the screen or on disk. For more information on document summaries and how to print them, refer to your WordPerfect manual.

7.2 Controlling the Printing Process

As you may have noticed, WordPerfect uses *background printing*. This means that you can continue to work with other documents while WordPerfect is printing. You can also print more than one document at a time. This is possible because WordPerfect creates a *print job* every time you send a document to the printer.

The Control Printer option under `Print` in the Print menu enables you to access the Printer Control screen. This is where WordPerfect manages the print jobs and where you can adjust the printing process.

Let's activate this option now. First activate Print by pressing `Shift`+`F7` or selecting Print from the File menu. Press `4` or `C` or click with the mouse to select Control Printer.

```
Print: Control Printer

Current Job

Job Number: None                          Page Number:  None
Status:     No print jobs                 Current Copy: None
Message:    None
Paper:      None
Location:   None
Action:     None


Job List

Job  Document              Destination        Print Options




Additional Jobs Not Shown: 0
```

The Printer Control screen

This screen lists information about the current print job and all the print jobs that are currently waiting to be printed. Also, at the bottom of the screen there is a list of options. You can use these options to cancel any of the print jobs, move a print job ahead of the others, display the entire list of jobs in the job list, restart the printer and stop the printer.

Initializing the printer

Another option listed under `Print` in the Print menu is Initialize Printer. This option is used when you want to use "soft fonts" with your printer. These fonts are software that must be sent from the computer to the printer in order to use them during the printing process. The Initialize Printer option enables you to "download" (send) the fonts to the printer. For more information on fonts, consult your WordPerfect manual.

Displaying the document

The View Document option, which we've previously discussed, is also located under `Print` in the Print menu. As you already know, this option enables you to see how your document will look when it is printed. This option is useful for ensuring that a document is properly formatted before printing it.

7.3 Printing Options

As we mentioned earlier, the Print screen is divided into two sections. Now that we've discussed the options that affect the actual printing process, let's discuss the options that will affect how the printed document will look. We'll only briefly discuss these options because most of them are advanced functions that aren't needed by a beginner.

The first option that is listed is Select Printer. The printer that is currently being used is listed next to this option. Let's activate this option now by pressing ⑤ or by clicking with the mouse.

```
Print: Select Printer

* Standard Printer




















```

Activating Select Printer

As you can see, the Print: Select Printer screen appears. The printers that were defined during installation are displayed on the screen. Since we have only one printer file selected here, only one choice appears on our screen. However, if you have more than one printer selected, you can select a different printer by highlighting it and using the Select option at the bottom of the Print: Select Printer screen.

The other options listed at the bottom of the screen enable you to install other printers (Additional Printers), edit the printer information (Edit), make a copy of an existing printer definition (Copy) and delete a printer definition (Delete). Also, the Help option provides special information about the currently selected printer and the Update option enables you to update your printer resource files.

Now activate Cancel (F1) or Exit (F7) to return to the Print menu. The Binding Offset option should be used when you're creating a document that will be bound, such as a book. The setting entered in this option determines how much space should be left on either side of the binding (i.e., text is moved to the right on odd pages and to the left on even pages).

With the Number of Copies option you can select how many copies of the document should be printed. The Multiple Copies Generated by option lets you determine whether WordPerfect or the printer should generate additional copies of a document. If you work on a network that supports this option, selecting the Printer setting can increase the speed of the printing process.

The last two options, Graphics Quality and Text Quality determine the resolution that will be used by your printer when printing graphics and text. Select the Graphics Quality option by pressing G or clicking with the mouse.

```
┌────────────────────────────────────────────────────────────────────────┐
│Print                                                                     │
│                                                                          │
│        1 - Full Document                                                 │
│        2 - Page                                                          │
│        3 - Document on Disk                                              │
│        4 - Control Printer                                               │
│        5 - Multiple Pages                                                │
│        6 - View Document                                                 │
│        7 - Initialize Printer                                            │
│                                                                          │
│                                                                          │
│Options                                                                   │
│                                                                          │
│        S - Select Printer                    Standard Printer            │
│        B - Binding Offset                    0"                          │
│        N - Number of Copies                  1                           │
│        U - Multiple Copies Generated by      WordPerfect                 │
│        G - Graphics Quality                  Medium                      │
│        T - Text Quality                      High                        │
│                                                                          │
│                                                                          │
│  .                                                                       │
│                                                                          │
│                                                                          │
│Graphics Quality: 1 Do Not Print; 2 Draft; 3 Medium; 4 High; 3           │
└────────────────────────────────────────────────────────────────────────┘
```

Activating Graphics Quality

As you can see, a list of options is displayed at the bottom of the screen. (The same options will appear when you activate the Text Quality option.) Use the Do Not Print option when your printer cannot print both graphics and text simultaneously. The options Draft, Medium and High determine the print quality that will be used to print the graphics or text. The higher quality that is used, the better the resolution. However, using higher quality also means that the printing process will take longer.

7.4 The List Files Feature

Another way to print documents that are on disk is by using the List Files feature. Let's try doing this now. First we must clear the screen. To do this, activate Exit ([F7] or Exit from the File menu) until you reach the normal editing screen and press [N] twice.

Now activate List Files by pressing [F5] or by selecting List Files from the File menu. Then press [Enter] to list the files that are located in the current directory (this is where your sample documents should be located). If your sample documents are located in a different directory, enter the name of the appropriate directory in the status line and press [Enter] . Your screen should look similar to the following:

```
07-10-91  11:52p            Directory C:\*.*
Document size:       0  Free: 10,960,896 Used:      720,332    Files:       14

.     Current    <Dir>                  ..    Parent     <Dir>
DEMO     .        <Dir> 05-20-91 02:29a  DEMO2    .       <Dir> 05-20-91 02:32a
DOS      .        <Dir> 03-11-91 02:17a  HIJAAK1  .       <Dir> 03-15-91 03:34a
HSG      .        <Dir> 05-07-91 05:46a  LAPLINK  .       <Dir> 03-13-91 03:56a
NETWARE  .        <Dir> 06-26-91 12:42p  NORTDESK.        <Dir> 06-27-91 09:39a
QB45     .        <Dir> 06-10-91 06:48a  SSTEMP   .       <Dir> 06-27-91 10:52a
WINDOWS  .        <Dir> 05-17-91 08:53a  WP51     .       <Dir> 03-13-91 03:56a
AUTOEXEC.BAT        107 05-17-91 09:03a  AUTOEXEC.NDW        107 05-17-91 09:03a
BALANCE  .        1,816 06-27-91 09:56p  BTINST   .EXE 529,119 05-29-91 05:27p
COMMAND  .COM    47,845 04-09-91 05:00a  CONFIG   .SYS     170 05-17-91 03:43p
HIMEM    .SYS    11,304 05-01-90 03:00a  LAPLINK  .TRE      80 03-15-91 03:34a
MIRROR   .BAK    50,688 06-05-91 06:50a  MIRROR   .FIL  50,688 06-05-91 07:09a
PROGRAMS.        17,219 07-01-91 11:37a  QB       .INI      48 06-13-91 08:36a
QUARTER  .        1,792 07-10-91 11:32p  WINA20   .386   9,349 04-09-91 05:00a
```

Activating List Files

Now move the cursor to the filename BALANCE and select the Print option by pressing [4] or [P]. Then press [Enter] to print the entire

189

document. After the * Please wait * message flashes briefly on the screen, the document will be printed.

This concludes our discussion of printing in WordPerfect. You should now have the essential information that is needed in order to print your own WordPerfect documents. As you use the Print feature more, you'll have a better understanding of the various options and how to use them.

The following tables list the key combinations and menu options of commands discussed in this section.

Action	Key combination
Block	[Alt]+[F4]
List files	[F5]
Print	[Shift]+[F7]
Print document on disk	[Shift]+[F7],[3]
	[Shift]+[F7],[D]
Retrieve document	[Shift]+[F10]
View document	[Shift]+[F7],[6]
	[Shift]+[F7],[V]

Action	Menu selection
Block	Edit/Block
List files	File/List Files
Print	File/Print
Print disk file	File/Print/Document on Disk
Retrieve document	File/Retrieve
View document	File/Print/View Document

Index

Abacus pc catalog

Order Toll Free 1-800-451-4319

5370 52nd Street SE • Grand Rapids, MI 49512
Phone: (616) 698-0330 • Fax: (616) 698-0325

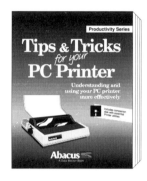
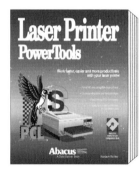

DOS 5.0 Complete

Not just another reference book - **DOS 5.0 Complete** is a practical user's guide to learning and using Microsoft's new DOS. It's an encyclopedia of DOS knowledge not only for the computer whiz but for the everyday user.

DOS 5.0 Complete is loaded with helpful hints for outfitting any computer with MS-DOS 5.0. From installing DOS 5.0 to using the new features for file, directory and storage maintenance you'll find techniques and hints here.

DOS 5.0 Complete has dozens of easy to follow examples. This book explains AUTOEXEC.BAT and CONFIG.SYS. The detailed explanations make this the most authoritative DOS book available. The friendly, easy to understand writing style insures that even beginners will grasp the fundamentals quickly and easily. And you'll find a complete DOS command reference.

Topics include:

- Learn the "ins and outs" of using the new MS-DOS 5.0
- Boost your productivity with these practical techniques
- Discover ways to solve your own DOS problems
- Save valuable time with the ready-to-run companion disk.
- Browse the extensive MS-DOS reference section
- Using DOS' new memory management features
- Using the improved SHELL ;for performing your computer housekeeping ;chores
- Using the new DOSKEY utility for faster command line editing and macro power.
- Using EDIT, the new full-screen editor
- Using QBASIC, DOS' new BASIC programming language
- Complete DOS command reference.

DOS 5.0 Complete includes a companion disk with example batch files, detailed explanations, and powerful tips and tricks to help you get the most out of MS-DOS 5.0. **DOS 5.0 Complete** will become THE source for reference information about DOS 5.0.

DOS 5.0 Complete
Authors: Michael Tornsdorf, Helmut Tornsdorf
ISBN 1-55755-109-X.
Suggested retail price $34.95 with companion disk.

DOS 5.0 Essentials

is the fast and effective way to learn the MS-DOS 5.0 operating system quickly and easily. Shows how you can operate DOS on a daily basis - from deleting and restoring files to generating macros to using commands and parameters. Using the menu-oriented DOS Shell makes operating system management even easier, right down to fast access to the DOS command line. Topics include: working with files, directories at a glance, storage media - diskettes and hard disks, using the DOS Shell and Program Manager, using the DOS command line, DOS Editor and more.
Author: Kelmens Mai
ISBN 1-55755-115-4. $14.95

GeoWorks Ensemble Now!

is your guide to the new graphic interface for PC XT, AT and 386 machines will make your computing life easier. **GeoWorks Ensemble Now!** is the fast and effective way to start using GeoWorks Ensemble immediately. This book features tutorials and concise summaries including: Window management, Applications in GeoWorks Ensemble, GeoManager, Data exchange in GeoWorks Ensemble, Using "normal" MS-DOS applications and much more.

Including:
- Installation
- General Skills
- Applications in GeoWorks Ensemble
- GeoManager
- More about GeoWorks Ensemble

Available August.
Author: R. Albrecht and M. Plurg
ISBN 1-55755-120-0. $12.95

To order direct call Toll Free 1-800-451-4319

In US and Canada add $5.00 shipping and handling. Foreign orders add $13.00 per item.
Michigan residents add 4% sales tax.

Virus Secure for Windows

Eliminate potential valuable data loss and minimize your risks with Virus Secure.

Don't give viruses the chance to ruin your data when you're using Windows. Avoid virus infection and potential valuable data loss. **Virus Secure for Windows** provides complete data protection for your hard and/or floppy disks from computer virus infection. **Virus Secure** is written by virus authority Ralf Burger (author of <u>Computer Viruses and Data Protection</u>). This is security that will keep your data alive and your PC operations productive.

Virus Secure can be run by both beginning and experienced users. Beginners will like the clear user interface and detailed error system. Experts will like the numerous options offered by **Virus Secure.** Beginning and advanced users will learn how to protect their diskettes and hard drives from unwanted data loss caused by viruses.

Virus Secure can detect over 200 known viruses and has built-in power for recognizing new or unknown viruses. It can also distinguish "normal" changes from "unusual" changes that viruses can make. **Virus Secure** can also be expanded. You can easily expand the recognition of viruses using a standard word processor. **Virus Secure** allows you to stay up to date as new viruses appear in the PC community.

Item #S108, ISBN 1-55755-108-1. Retail price $95.00.
System requirements: PC AT, 386 or compatible, hard drive and Windows 3.0.
Windows not included.

Author Ralf Burger

Windows is a trademark of Microsoft Corporation.

MICROSOFT WINDOWS

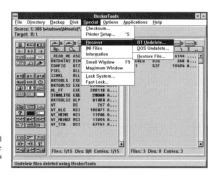

Name	
Address	

City		State	Zip

Country		Phone or FAX

Qty.	Title	Price

Payment:
- ☐ Visa
- ☐ Master Card
- ☐ American Express
- ☐ Check/ M.O.

Subtotal	
Michigan residents add 4% sales tax	
In US and Canada add $5.00 Shipping per order	
Foreign orders add $13.00 Shipping & Handling per item	
TOTAL amount enclosed (U.S. funds)	

Card No.

Exp. Date

Signature

PLEASE HELP US

So that we better understand who you are and what types of books interest you, please answer the following questions and return this prepaid card to us. THANK YOU!

Computer:
- ☐ IBM/ PC or compatible
- ☐ Commodore 64
- ☐ Macintosh
- ☐ PC/ AT or compatible
- ☐ Commodore 128
- ☐ Atari ST
- ☐ PC 386/ 486
- ☐ Amiga
- ☐ Other _____

I purchase most computer books from:
- ☐ Retail book store
- ☐ Retail computer store
- ☐ Discount book store
- ☐ Discount computer store
- ☐ Mail order
- ☐ Publisher direct

I learned of this book from:
- ☐ Magazine ad
- ☐ Store display rack
- ☐ Book review
- ☐ Catalog/ Brochure
- ☐ Recommendation
- ☐ Library

Suggestions for new books: _____

This book's title: _____

Comments: _____
_____

Your name: _____

Your company _____

Address: _____

City: _____ State: _____ Zip: _____

Purchased from (store name): _____

City: _____ State: _____ Zip: _____

Available Book Titles for IBM PC and Compatibles

Title	Price		Title	Price
Assembly Language -Step By Step w/2 disks	$34.95		PC and Compatibles for Beginners	$18.95
BASIC Programming Inside & Out w/disk	$34.95		PC Paintbrush Complete	$16.95
Batch File PowerTools w/disk	$34.95		PC System Programming w/2disks	$59.95
COBOL for Beginners	$18.95		Programming VGA Graphics w/2 disks	$39.95
Computers & Visual Stress	$12.95		QuickBASIC for Beginners	$18.95
Computer Viruses and Data Protection	$19.95		QuickBASIC Toolbox w/disk	$34.95
dBase IV for Beginners	$18.95		Stepping Up to DR DOS 6.0	$14.95
DOS 5.0 Complete w/disk	$34.95		Take Off with Flight Simulator	$16.95
DOS 5.0 Essentials	$14.95		The Leisure Suit Larry Story	$14.95
DOS 5.0 for Beginners	$18.95		Toolbook Now!	$12.95
Finding (Almost) Free Software	$16.95		Tips & Tricks PC Printer w/disk	$34.95
GEOWorks Ensemble Now!	$12.95		Turbo Pascal System Programming w/2 disks	$44.95
GW BASIC for Beginners	$18.95		UNIX for Beginners	$18.95
Kings Quest Saga	$14.95		UNIX/XENIX Reference Guide	$ 9.95
Laser Printer Powertools w/disk	$34.95		Upgrading and Maintaining Your PC	$24.95
Lotus 1-2-3 for Beginners	$18.95		Windows System Programming w/disk	$39.95
MS-DOS for Beginners	$18.95		Word 5.0/5.5 Powertools w/disk	$34.95
Novell Netware Simplified	$24.95		Word for Windows Know How w/disk	$34.95
Paradox 3.5 Now	$12.95		Word for Windows Powertools w/disk	$34.95

To order call **TOLL FREE 1-800-451-4319** in US and Canada

NO POSTAGE
NECESSARY
IF MAILED
IN THE
UNITED STATES

BUSINESS REPLY MAIL
FIRST-CLASS MAIL PERMIT NO 5504 GRAND RAPIDS MI

POSTAGE WILL BE PAID BY ADDRESSEE

Abacus
5370 52nd St SE
Grand Rapids MI 49502-8107